Unconditional

Monica
May your life be filled with unconditional love

Nycki
~2005

STAY TUNED FOR THE UPCOMING STONE TRILOGY

from Nycki Whiting

Grieving a Rolling Stone© 2006

Semi-Precious Stone© 2007

Diamond in the Rough© 2008

FOR MORE INFORMATION CONSULT:
http://home.comcast.net/~nyckiwhiting1/love.html

Nycki Whiting

Unconditional

A Collection of Inspirational Stories, With Poems by Melanie White Eley and Shonda Rowe

1663 Liberty Drive, Suite 200
Bloomington, Indiana 47403
(800) 839-8640
www.AuthorHouse.com

Except for Troubled, these stories are fictional. References to real events, businesses, organizations, and locales are intended only to give the fictional sense of reality. Any resemblance to actual persons, living or dead is entirely coincidental. In Troubled, the names of the characters have been changed. However, every other aspect of Troubled is true.

© 2005 Nycki Whiting. All Rights Reserved.

No part of this book may be reproduced, stored in a retrieval system, or transmitted by any means without the written permission of the author.

First published by AuthorHouse 10/25/05

ISBN: 1-4208-9328-9 (sc)

Printed in the United States of America
Bloomington, Indiana

This book is printed on acid-free paper.

Front cover design by Ryan Elizabeth Pack

ACKNOWLEDGMENTS

Thanks to Corlice Arnold, Cheryl Basye, David Byrd, Rosette Hunter, Shirley Kinsey, Ray Lerer, Lucy Livingston, Beverly Lyle, Shonda Rowe, Father LeBaron Taylor, Juette Elaine Taylor, and Alice Wyatt for being my friends, for giving me the opportunity to read my stories aloud to you, and for reading version after version of all of these stories. Thanks to everybody who ain't Willie Clemons but still listened to endless discussions about my writings. Special thanks to Henrietta Spearman and Yvonne Wiltz who have done all of the above and more. Thanks for being my girls.

Melanie and Shonda, thank you for allowing me to share your poetic talents with the world. Joyce Wells, words can not express the extent of my gratitude. Thank you for your inspiration, contributions, and tenaciousness in "encouraging" me to complete this project, the Stone Trilogy and my timesheets.

Ryan Elizabeth Pack, thank you for being my baby girl, allowing me to use the image of you and your son on the cover, and most of all, for giving birth to Carter, my precious grandson. Thank you Jordan Wilson Pack, your presence in my life forced me to acknowledge my emotions. Many of them are expressed in this book. Deborah Linda Whiting Sprow and Dorothy "Grace" Whiting McQueen, thank you for being proud of me, reading my stories, bragging about me shamelessly, and for being my sisters. Thank you for loving me. Thank you, Mom, Dorothy Elizabeth Wilson Whiting, (whose name really wasn't Dorothy) and Darnell Grace Whiting Mahdiah, for looking down from heaven and providing protection and inspiration. Darnell, Carter got your message. I love you all, unconditionally.

Honey bunny, publicly known as Michael R. Pack, what can I say. By filling in the cracks of our life together, you gave me the time and space to pursue my writing. Thank you for being my agent, my marketing expert, my scheduler, my accountant, my angel investor and my everything. Without you, neither this book nor the wonderful life that we have built together would be possible. Thank you so very much for loving me, unconditionally.

Finally, I want to thank the Supreme Being for inspiring me to find my voice and discover the gift of writing that was bestowed on me.

This book is dedicated to my son, M. Jordan Wilson Pack, and all those who are assisting us in bringing him into manhood. May God deploy an army of Guardian Angels to protect him from himself and all those who seek to destroy him.

Contents

Author's Notes
xi

The Visit
3

The Breakup
15

Second Thoughts
37

Setting a Screen
69

Troubled: A True Story
107

Coral's Apology
(excerpt from Grieving a Rollin' Stone)
153

1 Corinthian 13
169

AUTHOR'S NOTES

The Ages of Unconditional Love

When I was **10**, unconditional love smelled like coffee with lots and lots of Pet Milk® and lots and lots of sugar. The kind I used to drink while sitting on the small porch of our Detroit bungalow with my mother. The same kind that I now drink daily in the form of a Starbucks® iced, Grande, latte, decaf, soy with two sweeteners. Whenever my mother let me drink coffee with her while we kept our feet up on the railing so that our ankles wouldn't swell, I knew I was loved. Of course, my ankles never swelled. However, my mother who, in hindsight, seemed to be pregnant an awful lot during my childhood, had numerous problems with her ankles, her sugar and the poison levels in her blood. I can never remember what that is called. But I can remember how those therapeutic days felt and how that coffee smelled.

When I was **20**, unconditional love sounded like the melodious voice of Chaka Khan and Rufus warming up for the invincible sound of Earth, Wind, and Fire. Chaka was smaller and younger then and so was I. Sitting on the lawn at Pine Knob, a ski mountain turned concert venue for the summer, drinking wine with that young, engineering student who had put a quarter karat diamond on the correct finger, on the correct hand, at what I thought was the correct time in my life, I knew I was loved. It must have all been correct because I am still listening to music in open air venues with that student turned man who, on our thirtieth wedding anniversary, replaced the round cut diamond with a three karat marquise.

When I was **30**, unconditional love felt like the softness of that baby girl who I had birthed a year earlier. Her long slim body, her latte colored skin and her consistent need to be wherever I was, was heartwarming and draining at the same time. Whenever she smiled at me or wrapped her soft arms around my neck or told me "I lub you, Mommy," I knew I was loved. And I know I'm loved now when I hear those same words from her son. He tells me everyday, even though he's not talking yet.

*When I was **40**, unconditional love looked like that little boy who was not a part of my body but an immense part of my heart, my soul and my family. Whenever, in the midst of our ups and downs, he would curl up next to me and give me a wet kiss on my cheek, I knew I was loved. By the time he was fifteen, standing six-feet, three inches tall, it was nasty to curl up with his mom. Instead he showed his love by kissing me on the forehead and buying, before its release date, with his own money, and without my requesting, Queen Latifah's Beauty Shop DVD.*

*But by the time I made **50**, my mother had passed away; my husband, though still attentive, had found respite in golf and playing with his grandson; and my children had begun their own quest for unconditional love. It was in that serenity of middle age that I realized that love is best smelled, heard, felt, seen and tasted by effectuating a love for God, myself and for others that is . . .*

Unconditional

Unconditional

The Visit

In Memory of Christopher Lewis

My heart aches with pain
Every tear seems so in vain
I need to talk to that love one once again
I need to resolve some things within

There is a place where we can meet
A place where my soul can be at peace
A place that is undisturbed
A place where answers can be heard

My love is all I ever wanted to express
From my heart to yours is where it's kept
But we must keep this love in a sacred place
Somewhere pure – somewhere chaste

Pain is an emotion that we all feel
But there is no pain that love can not heal

© 2005 Shonda Rowe

She looked so glorious and so serene; far more serene than she was when I last saw her five years earlier and far too serene for the woman who had acquired the title of the "oldest, loudest and latest" sister. Just the sight of her was soothing to my soul. She had appeared out of nowhere. My first thought was that she was an angel. But I didn't see a halo circling her head. Nor was there a glow surrounding her body.

"Hello Eshe," she said.

"Nia, where have you been? How are you doing? How did you get here?" I asked hardly catching a breath in between the sentences and wanting to know all of the answers instantly.

She didn't answer. I attempted to hug her but she avoided my touch. A puzzled look crossed her face. Her hair cascaded halfway down her back. The silkiness of each loose ringlet glistened in the sunlight of the beautiful garden in which we were standing. I reached again; this time attempting to move a ringlet from her eye. She pulled away again.

I don't remember what I was doing or where I was prior to her appearance. However when she arrived, I was standing under a magnolia tree waiting for her as if she was expected. I was holding my normally energetic eight-month old grandson, Bakari, who became immediately mesmerized with his great aunt. His face broke into a brilliant smile and, for the first time since his birth, Bakari was perfectly still.

"I came to see the newest member of our family," Nia responded.

I held him out for her to take but she moved away. She had always been a large woman, standing six-feet tall and weighing in the neighborhood of two hundred and fifty pounds. Yet, despite her size, she seemed to be floating. Her loose fitting white blouse fell off one shoulder as she glided down the brick walkway. The gentle wind caused her long white skirt to trail slightly behind her.

I followed her oblivious to the array of pink, yellow and purple flowers lining the walkway and interspersed throughout the garden. I once heard that it angers God when people don't notice color. The tranquility of that day is proof that God was not annoyed. Branches of wisteria trees hung over head and protected us from the sun beaming down. The smell of honeysuckle invaded the air.

Nia moved quickly. She didn't speak.

"Do you remember when we were kids and you use to tell me that you were going to suck my sweet face because I was your honeysuckle?" I said hoping to ease the mystery.

Nia smiled but still didn't respond. Her pace quickened and suddenly she was almost out of sight.

"Please hurry Eshe. I don't want to waste a minute," she said.

"Why are you in such a hurry?"

"She has to get back," Bakari responded.

I stopped in my tracks and almost dropped him to the ground. He had not grown in size; however, his face looked like that of a very mature, miniature adult. His mouth was full of teeth. His straight jet black hair was now curly brown locks identical to those that cascaded down Nia's back.

The panic that was forming inside of me subsided when he looked at me with his big brown eyes and said, "I love you, Ya-Ya."

I pulled his small body close. He wrapped his arms around my neck and laid his head on my shoulder. As I followed Nia into the gazebo at the end of the path, a quiet peace came over me. Calmness was omnipresent.

Nia sat on the bench in the gazebo so that the sun was behind her. She gracefully waved her arm in the air motioning for me to sit next to her. Then I saw it; the glow and the halo. Instantaneously I knew the circumstances of the last time I actually saw her. It was just minutes, no seconds before the minister closed her coffin.

I also remembered how angry I was with her then. I wasn't angry at her for dying and leaving me and my two sisters one year after our mother and two years after our grandmother had done the same. No, I was mad at her for not believing in herself and fighting to stay alive. It was almost as if she willed herself to death. In my mind, she might have well committed suicide. I couldn't accept what she had done.

Overtime however, I came to understand that during her life Nia could never make peace with herself for the blunders of her teen years and her young adult life. These blunders followed and inhibited her until her death at fifty-four years of age. Maybe "blunder" isn't a strong enough word for promiscuity and drug addiction. Maybe her actions were more like mistakes . . . huge mistakes. However, they were just that, mistakes made by a child who herself was a mistake of a spontaneous sexual encounter between two teens.

Not only did our parents blame Nia for all of her

mistakes, they also blamed her for being the origin of the ill-fated relationship that they called a marriage. That blame caused tension that lead to Nia's pain. My sisters and I thought that if she would just stop getting in trouble, the screaming would subside, the tension would go away and everything would be alright. At the time, none of us, not even Nia, realized that she wasn't the cause of the tension. In fact, her acting out was actually her response. Over time she erected a shield to provide a safe haven from the pain. That shield repelled our love and we, at least my sisters and I, truly loved her.

I like to think that I had begun to break into Nia's shell during our long telephone conversations that occurred just before her death. I think my sisters feel that they also found cracks in Nia's armor. We all know, however, that her heart was opened by Rashad, her husband who preceded her in death. Until I saw her sitting there in the sun, I didn't remember her earlier visits or how, with her help, I had all but resolved my issues with her death. I now understood that her willed death was her way of reuniting with the only person that she felt truly loved her during her life. I needed to know that she was still with Rashid.

"Nia, where's Rashid?" I asked.

A big smile covered her face. I had watched the funeral director place his ashes in her coffin. I was delighted to know that act had successfully kept them together and hoped they would be together for all times. I felt another surge of peace.

"Nia..." I started to tell her that we loved her now and had always loved her. I also wanted to tell her that whether or not our parents forgave her wasn't important because God had forgiven her. Before I could get the words out, I realized that they didn't need to be said. She obviously already knew. After all, she had come to see the newest member of our family . . . my first grandchild.

"Come sit next to me. Let me talk to your beautiful grandson."

I did as she requested.

"Bakari! What a wonderful name for you. I am your Great Aunt Nia. I've come a long way to meet you. Do you know why? I came because I love you very much. You must always know that, no matter what, I will love you and I will always be with you."

"Thank you for that assurance, Aunt Nia. I love you too," Bakari responded.

"But more importantly Bakari, God loves you and he has great promise for you, a boy whose name means promise," Nia continued.

I was sitting right there, right next to Nia with Bakari in my lap. However, I have no memory of the rest of their conversation which went on for hours. Nia abruptly stood up, turned to me and said, just as she had done at the end of all our previous visits, "Asante sana kwa upendo wako."

Then, just as suddenly as she had appeared, she was gone. I wanted to yell for her to stay a little longer but I knew she couldn't. I longed for a hug or a touch but in one of her previous visits she had explained that wasn't possible.

Nature's noises which had been stilled during her visit, abruptly restarted. I pulled Bakari close to me and kissed his forehead. He was once again the eight-month old that I found hard to contain. I remained in the gazebo, fearful that leaving would terminate the remaining tranquility of the garden.

Several hours later, I woke up. I went into Bakari's

room and found my daughter standing over his bed smiling at her sleeping child.

"Your Aunt Nia came to visit me last night," I exclaimed.

I had always advised my children to welcome visits from loved ones who had gone to the other side.

I guess that is why, without hesitation, Hakima responded "so that is who Bakari was talking to last night. I knew it had to be something special going on because he has never before talked in his sleep. Plus, I thought I made out the world 'love.'"

It was then that I knew for sure that Nia's visit was not a dream. I also realized exactly why Nia had come. She not only wanted to meet her great nephew. She also wanted to assure Bakari, the child of my unwed daughter's failed relationship, that he was loved unconditionally.

Swahili Translations

Eshe – Love
Nia – Purpose
Bakari – Promise
YaYa – Grandmother
Rashid – Wise One
Hakima – Sensible

Asante sana kwa mapenzi yenu.

Thank you for loving me.

The Breakup

Because in you I saw,
my children
my home
my future
my life
my strength
my reason.
Is it really a wonder that
since you've been gone, I can no longer see my dreams?

©1992 Melanie White Eley

*T*he heat in the small, dark bedroom of my Cambridge apartment was stifling. I could hardly breathe. His massive body hovered over me. The stare of his red pupils pierced my soul. His voice was bellowing. He moved closer. I knew he was demanding an answer, although I couldn't understand the words he was roaring at me. Several times he mentioned her name but I didn't understand why. He continued to move his repulsive face closer until it was only inches from mine. The closer he came the hotter I got.

Eventually, the heat became unbearable. With his mouth only inches from my face he again demanded a response. Fearing that he was only seconds away from causing me bodily harm or that the heat would cause me to have a stroke, I screamed "yes." The scream awakened me but I did not immediately open my eyes fearing that he was still in the room. When I finally eased them open, the room was pitch black. There was no one there. Relief replaced my fear but it was quickly displaced by the omnipresent piercing of my broken heart.

I wanted that intense experience to be the culmination of a bad dream. Maybe, just maybe, the entire last month was part of that same bad dream. Maybe, instead of becoming a recluse, I had actually been out enjoying this last summer before I became a gainfully employed adult. Maybe, just maybe, Victoria had not left our law school graduation ceremony, packed her belongings and boarded a plane for Atlanta. Maybe she still really loved me and was on her way home right now. Maybe! Maybe not.

But there was no maybe about the way I felt about her. I loved her unconditionally although I was angry, hurt, afraid and confused. Twelve years earlier we promised each other that we would always be together. We promised to support each other and encourage each other through high school, college and law school. We vowed that we would become high powered Wall Street attorneys but that wouldn't stop us from having a wonderful family and a great home in the country. The fact that, before we even met, we both wanted to be Wall Street attorneys was testament to the fact that we were made for each other. We had so many other things in common we knew and individually thanked God for letting us find our soul mate at such an early age.

At first our parents tolerated the relationship with skepticism. Both sets feared that our closeness would interfere with their desires for us to capitalize on our respective tremendous intelligence. However, when we both applied and were accepted to an Ivy League school in the northeast, they too were convinced that this was a match made in heaven. Besides few working class parents would protest their children attending Harvard. Their only admonishment was that we not live together.

Of course, we didn't comply. At the end of our freshmen year, we found an apartment a short distance from campus and secured it with a deposit. When we returned to Cambridge for our sophomore year we moved in together. When we got accepted into Harvard Law, we considered moving on campus but that would have required us to live apart. That wasn't happening and so we stayed in our apartment. At least, I stayed.

Victoria moved on to focus on her career goals that were nothing like those that we had been discussing and aiming at for years. When we entered our third year of law school, everything was on track. However, without my knowledge, she declined an offer from a prestigious Wall Street firm where she worked the previous summer. Instead, she clandestinely secured an alternate position with a boutique firm in Atlanta. Immediately after the graduation ceremony she told me about the change in plans. I offered to come with her. She said that wasn't necessary. I offered to give her space if that was what she needed. I would be making enough money to visit her monthly and she could also visit me in New York. She again said that wasn't necessary.

In an act of desperation, I pulled out of my pocket the engagement ring that I had planned to present to her at a quiet dinner following the reception that our parents were throwing. I had previously disclosed the dinner plans to our parents. Delighted with the idea, they had agreed to host a short, joint but elegant reception for the family members who had traveled to Cambridge to attend the graduation. Both mothers thought the ring was gorgeous. My mother was proud I made such a wise selection. Her mother was proud her daughter would be sporting a three karat diamond.

However, Victoria didn't think much of the ring or the plan. When I flipped the black velvet box open, revealing the sparking solitaire marquise diamond peeking out of the red velvet lining, she turned to me and without expression said, "No. I don't want to marry you. I don't love you. As I said, I am going to Atlanta to focus on my career. That is what is important to me now." She left and I attended the reception alone.

I called her several times from the reception and her

family called as well. Her response to me was, "Please accept what I said and let me go without drama." Her response to her family was, "I love you. I am sorry. This is something I have to do. I'm OK and I'll see you soon."

The first time our parents asked me what was going on, I responded accurately, "I have no idea." The second time they asked, I broke down in tears. My brother escorted me out of the reception, to this apartment where I've stayed almost exclusively for an entire month.

My family returned to Detroit shortly after the graduation and whenever they called, I managed to muster enough composure to convince them that I was getting along alright. The few friends who remained in Cambridge knew I was not. They checked on me several times a day. They brought food and poured out the liquor which was the only thing I left the apartment to buy. They attempted to get me out of the apartment initially to go to parties and then to go to counseling, but I would not move. I didn't bathe or brush my teeth for days at a time. That dream, that horrible, horrible dream made me realize that I needed to get a hold of myself.

Riding solo, I agonizingly implemented as much of our plan as possible. I packed my belongings and moved to New York in preparation for my career as a high powered Wall Street lawyer. Living off of the large signing bonus provided by the firm in June, I spent the remainder of that summer drinking, partying and crying. When September arrived and it was time to start working. I welcomed the diversion. I worked fifteen hours a day, seven days a week and when I wasn't working, I was still drinking, partying and crying. I still loved Victoria.

Unconditional

I wanted to call her everyday but I resisted. She had asked me to let her go and I was determined to honor her wishes. By Thanksgiving, I thought that enough time had passed for me to call her and wish her happy holidays. For days I practiced what I would say to her. I fantasized that once she heard my voice she would automatically melt; recant her graduation speech and come running home to me. That didn't happen.

She answered her office telephone on the first ring. I hoped that it was because she recognized the area code and knew it was me. It wasn't. Instead, she was waiting for a call from co-counsel on a big case. Although she was in a hurry, she was cordial. We talked about our jobs, the weather in our respective parts of the country, and our new apartments. After fifteen minutes, she thanked me for calling and hung up. I secretly wished she would lose the case. For the next week, I forgot the partying and just engaged in working, drinking, crying and feeling guilty for wishing bad luck on her.

A few days after the conversation, one of our mutual friends from Harvard Law called to tell me that Victoria had been released from her law firm because she committed serious errors that caused her to lose the case she was working on when I called. Although I smiled on the inside, I felt bad for her. We had been together long enough for me to know that she was depressed. I thought that maybe I should call to console her. Maybe this would be the thing that would send her back to me. I didn't call and she didn't come back. Instead she immediately secured another job with a securities firm in Atlanta. After all, not only had we graduated from Harvard Law, we graduated at the top of our class.

Over the next year, my commitment to my firm became even more intense. I cut out the partying, increased the drinking and stopped the crying but the sorrow remained. No matter how hard I tried not to, I still loved her. I promised myself that this holiday season I would not call her. Maybe, just maybe she would call me. She didn't. On Christmas Eve, I decided that I needed to be with loved ones on the holiday. At great cost, I bought a round trip ticket to Detroit leaving that evening and returning early on the morning of the twenty-sixth. My firm was only closed one day and as a second year associate on the partnership track I was expected to be in my office the day after Christmas.

My parents were elated with my surprise visit. They understood that my work schedule was demanding and that it prevented me from coming home very often. What they didn't know was that, up until that day, the pain from memories of me and Victoria's days at Detroit's Cass Technical High School were more distressing than my need to be with my family.

To my surprise, they were having Christmas dinner with Victoria's parents. Apparently, since both couples were now empty nesters, they spent a lot of time together. I tried to get out of going to Victoria's family's house but my parents wouldn't hear of it. They went on and on about how great it was for me to be home and to join them at dinner. It was almost going to be like old times. Feeling trapped, I acquiesced. Before we left, I slipped in the bathroom to gather my strength and flush the tears so that my parents wouldn't know that, after all this time, I still loved Victoria.

No one understood Victoria's change of heart, least of all her parents. They, like everyone else who knew us, felt that God meant for us to be together. However, being good parents, they knew they could not press her into a relationship she didn't seem to want. However, as my parents told me, Victoria's parents considered me their son-in-law even though I wasn't married to her.

I don't remember which one of my corny parents thought it would be a good idea for me to go to the door by myself and surprise Victoria's parents with my presence. My father stopped the car in front of the house. As planned, when I got out, he drove up the street so they would think I had mysteriously arrived. I painfully walked the long walkway to the front porch of the small Tudor styled house. I had walked this way so many times before, with and without Victoria. This was the first time that I walked it in pain. It took all of the strength I could muster to keep from turning and running away. In the past, I would have walked in the door that was never locked without knocking. This time, I rang the door bell.

Waiting for someone to answer was excruciating. Finally, the door flew open and there in front of me was Victoria. We starred at each other for what seemed like forever. I envisioned her running to me, throwing her arms around my neck and apologizing profusely. She interrupted my fantasy when she asked, "Well are you going to come in?"

As soon as I entered the house, her parents surrounded me. They asked me questions about where I was working and what I was doing. Then they answered them. My parents had already told them the answers. Numerous other family members and friends entered the house while we were still in the hallway. Within minutes, the house was full of people and commotion. Victoria got lost in the crowd.

I spent most of the day trying to position myself

alone with Victoria although I was afraid of what she might say. I fantasized that we would get together in the beautiful gardens behind her house and that she would fall into my arms professing her love for me. Of course, that didn't happen, especially since it was December and we were in Detroit.

When we finally did get a chance to talk privately, it was in the living room just out of ear shot of people stirring around in the adjacent dining room. As she told me how much she enjoyed the people and the work at her new firm, sight unseen, I begin to hate all of them. I wished the firm would instantaneously dissolve leaving no remnant that it ever existed. I just knew that if she didn't have those stupid career goals, she would have never left me. After a few minutes, she stood and said it was great seeing me again and went into the other room to socialize.

I hoped that I would be able to convince her to go out for a ride or to visit some of our old friends that evening. I was really trying to give her as much opportunity as possible to profess her love to me. However, like me, she had to be at work on the twenty-sixth. Her plane for Atlanta left Detroit at seven o'clock in the evening on Christmas Day. She left her parents home at five o'clock without saying goodbye to me.

On the way back to my parent's house, I didn't want to talk to anyone about anything. My parents went on and on about how good Victoria looked and whether or not we had an opportunity to talk. I knew they wanted to ask more questions but they knew that it wasn't prudent for them to pry too deeply into my relationship. What they didn't seem to understand was that as far as Victoria was concerned there wasn't a relationship. I, of course, still loved her but was beginning to surmise that I needed to accept life without Victoria.

When we reached the house, I was exhausted. I had to get up at four o'clock the next morning to catch the plane back to New York. My parents understood my going directly to bed. I cried as I readied myself and then made myself a promise. That would be the last time I cried over that lost love. I was determined to bring in the New Year in New York with a different perspective. As soon as my head hit the pillow, I was asleep.

The room was dark except for the flames bellowing behind the head of the horrible creature. This time he was not screaming at me. Instead he was laughing wildly and pointing at me. Again he was spewing words that I couldn't understand. Every so often I would make out the word "Victoria." I opened my eyes and screamed "Victoria is not a part of my life and neither are you, devil. Stay away from me and my dreams."

The next day, when I arrived at my office in New York, I clicked onto the Wall Street Journal webpage to check the business news. Usually nothing much happened in the days between Christmas and New Years. Therefore, I was surprised to see the head lines which read:

ENTIRE ATLANTA FIRM INDICTED FOR SECURITIES FRAUD

I read further to discover it was Victoria's firm. Her name was among those indicted. My heart stopped and suddenly I understood the devil's words from the night before. He had been congratulating me on how I was coming along, and indicating how proud he was of me for destroying an entire firm instead of just one lawyer like I had done previously. As clear as day I heard him say, "You're going to prove to be one of my best minions."

My head was spinning. This couldn't be true. I couldn't have caused the break up of her firm. It was just coincidental. The dream was generated by my guilt for wishing bad on someone else. I was a good Catholic boy. I believed in guilt and oppression. Was the dissolution of her firm part of some deal I made with the devil? No. Hell no! I was determined I was not going to lose my mind over this. Victoria was involved in something that had nothing to do with me. I refused to let her misfortune cloud my good judgment.

However, as hard as I was trying to get a new perspective on life, I couldn't resist following the case. At one point, I thought about taking a leave of absence and going to Atlanta to volunteer to assist her defense team. Even though I had developed a reputation as one of the top contract attorneys on Wall Street, I didn't know a thing about criminal law, securities law or litigation. I still tried; I wanted to help her. Several times I called Victoria to offer. She would not accept my calls. Her attorneys brushed me off too. Finally, I wrote her a letter simply telling her that I was praying for her. She never wrote back.

The truth was that I wasn't praying for her or anybody. I couldn't. I hadn't been to church since I graduated from law school. Whenever I tried, I would suffer an anxiety attack that made me run, not walk, back to my apartment. Several times I knelt by my bed to pray but I couldn't because even that caused me to be engulfed with guilt.

Then when Victoria was found guilty of conspiracy and sentenced to twenty-four months in a prison, I lost the battle to maintain my sanity. I was thoroughly convinced that I had made a pact with the devil to destroy her career. I tried again to go to church and see if the priest could help me rid myself of the terrible curse. I needed and wanted to confess my sins, but the anxiety wouldn't stop. I never made it into the church.

Instead, I went to a psychologist so that he could help me rationalize my beliefs about the dreams. His therapy didn't work. In fact, the guilt got worst and the ever-present throbbing increased. Adding to the pain of my broken heart was my knowing that my selfishness caused her downfall. The time commitment required to become a top Wall Street attorney had taken a toll on my social relationships. My only friends were co-workers. I couldn't let them know how disturbed I was. With therapy not working, no one to talk to, and the pain and guilt increasing by the minute, I didn't know what to do. I walked out on the terrace of my Jersey apartment, climbed over the railing and let myself fall.

Several days later, I woke up to find my mother sitting in a chair next to my hospital bed. I tried to speak to her but there was a tube taped in my mouth. The first question out of my mouth after the tube was removed was, "where is Victoria?" I again was hoping that this hospital stay was the culmination of a bad dream. Maybe it was still the summer before I assumed my role as an adult. It wasn't and Victoria was in prison. When my mother asked if I jumped because of Victoria, I flinched and told her that I had fallen by accident.

Luckily, a canopy broke my fall and turned my body around so that I landed on my legs instead of my head. This apparently saved my life although I broke almost every bone in the lower half of my body. After a while my body began to heal and, surprisingly, so did my spirit. I was no longer ravished with guilt or a broken heart. I had no explanation for the change in my temperament but I appreciated the liberation. Now I would be able to finally find that new perspective.

The day before I was to be released from the hospital, a priest from a nearby parish visited me. I was pleased and surprised that I wasn't having an anxiety attack in his presence. When I requested that he hear my confession, he laughed and asked what could I have possibly done since I was brought into the hospital. He went on to tell me that immediately before going into the operating room, I demanded to see a priest. He heard my confession, gave me the last rites and absolved me of all my sins. He jokingly commented that because I had been in traction since that time, unless I had been having some awfully bad thoughts, my soul was pure as snow.

It took about a year for my body to heal completely. During that time, I took a leave of absence from my Wall Street firm and affiliated myself as of-counsel with a small firm in Detroit. Working part time gave me the flexibility to read, write and paint. The drinking, partying and crying were part of my past life. Although, the doctor recommended that I participate in therapy, I declined saying that I was fine. I convinced everyone that I did not jump from the patio; I fell and I was happy to be alive.

And I was truly happy and for the first time since Victoria left, I was at peace with myself. Occasionally, I thought about her but it was no longer painful and oppressive. I still loved her but felt no guilt for her misfortune. I realized that those dreams were just that . . . dreams. I accepted that our relationship, although it lasted twelve years was an "in the meantime" relationship. I needed to gather the lessons learned and move on.

That August, while I was sitting in my parent's backyard among the plethora of flowers that they planted every summer, my mother handed me a letter. She watched me intently as I read the envelope. It was from a women's prison in Virginia. When I looked up at my mother, she retreated back into the house, stopping to glance at me just before she entered the back door.

I held the letter in my hands for a long while wondering if I should open it or throw it away. Maybe Victoria was finally professing her love to me. Maybe this was just a get well note that would take me back to the agonizing place I had been before the . . . accident. I really didn't want to go back there. I knew that my mother was watching me through the kitchen window so I wanted to appear calm. Eventually curiosity got the best of me. I ripped the envelope open and snatched the letter out. It read:

Beloved:

    I hope this letter finds you in good spirits. My parents told me that you are recovering quite well and that you appear to be at peace with your circumstances. I am happy to hear that. With everything, I have been through in the last two years, amazingly, I am at peace too. At least, I am almost at peace. I have one more thing to do before I can achieve the complete and total tranquility that I desire.
    That one thing is to apologize to you. Despite what I said, I have always loved you and even now, I love you. When we graduated from law school I thought I was losing my mind and I didn't, no I couldn't, subject you to that. You wanted so badly to be a successful Wall Street attorney and you were so close. Your dreams would have been

destroyed if you had to care for an insane wife. I know you wouldn't have left me for any reason.

My turmoil began during our first year of law school. Of course, you remember how despondent you were after your sister died. Prior to that time, we had both been doing great. We were acing our classes and enjoying our life together. But when we returned from the funeral, everything changed. You were so broken up all you wanted to do was drink and sleep.

I must admit, I didn't quite understand the extent of your grief. Maybe that was because I didn't really understand your relationship with your sister. You two fought like cats and dogs. I always thought you hated each other. However, every time something bad happened to her, which seemed to be often, you would go into a deep depression as if you were somehow responsible. Most times you would pop back to your old self within a few days and then you two would be at each other again.

After her death, it didn't seem like you were ever going to shake your grief. I tried not to worry; thinking that you would eventually come around. After several months of your listlessness, I became concerned. After all, your grades were slipping and taking our dreams for the future with them. I researched grief on the internet and concluded that yours was unnatural.

Using my internet psychology I determined you had an adjustment disorder. You needed professional help to pull you out of your depression. But you refused to see a counselor. So I attempted to revive your spirit. But nothing I did seemed to work. I was desperate to find a way out for you.

Then I begin having this horrible dream. It really wasn't a recurring dream. It was more like a continuation dream. In the dream, I made a pack with the devil that he could have my soul if only

Unconditional

he would bring back the man I loved and help him become that high powered successful Wall Street attorney you had once longed to become. You eventually shook your depression and managed to finish our freshmen year in the top three percent of the class.

However, the bad dreams continued until the day before we graduated. At first, I thought they were nothing more than the result of eating late night snacks while studying. But after a while, they became real and I obsessed over the fact that I had become the devil's minion. I resented you for not knowing about my torment, although I never told you or anyone. You had no way of finding out.

I wanted to get even with you for taking my soul and not showing gratitude. I started wishing bad things would happen to you. Then when they happened, I thought I was responsible and felt guilty. I surmised that all of my bad thoughts came true because of my pact with the devil. I blamed myself for your car accident and for your graduating number two in our class instead of number one.

I tried going to a priest to confess hoping that would cleanse my soul but every time I got anywhere near the church, anxiety over took me. I would run away. That is why I never went to church with you. I also sought help from the school counselor but she laughed at me on the first visit. I never went back.

By the middle of our third year, I was practically deranged. That was the only time that I was glad that we had chosen to take different classes. Between studying, attending classes and our internships, we spent very little time together. I was able to conceal my mental state from you.

When I heard you had fallen off of your deck,

I literally lost my mind. I knew I was responsible for your fall. You see, when I saw you walking towards my parents' house, in my desperation not to face you, I wished you would lose your ability to walk. I know that sounds horrible. I thought you had walked from your parents' house to beg me to come back. I knew it would be difficult for me to resist. You see, being with you without being able to profess my love for you was painful. Actually, it was more than painful: it was oppressive.

Despite my efforts, I couldn't shake the belief that I had caused your fall. The guilt consumed me. Then finally, I couldn't take anymore. One evening, I went into my cell, tied the sheets together, threw them over the pipes running across the top of my cell and attempted to hang myself. I hung there for just a few minutes before the pipes broke and I fell to the ground. The guards heard the noise, found me unconscious on the floor and rushed me to the medical ward where I stayed heavily sedated for several weeks.

Although I have no memory of it, I'm told that during that time I demanded to see a priest and would not rest until he performed the last rites. Ironically, I was in no danger of dying. A few days later, I woke up in peace. The only thing that troubled me was that I had not apologized to you.

I know all of this sounds crazy but as God is my witness, it is absolutely true. I just hope that you can forgive me. Although, I know it is probably too late for us, I want you to know that I have always loved you and will always love you, unconditionally.

Victoria,

> PS: I will be released in a few months and placed in a halfway house in Detroit. If you are still there, I'll look you up.

I read the letter over several times in disbelief. Then I folded it neatly and put it in my pocket. I leaned back in the chaise lounge, closed my eyes and thought "Forgive you . . . absolutely. Still be in Detroit . . . absolutely. Too late for us… maybe . . . maybe not. … Love keeps no record of a suffered wrong."

The devil is in the details.

Second Thoughts

One day, a long time from now,
When the world has dealt us our cards,
delivered our blows.
When we are not so mentally young,
so idealistic, so foolish.
When we realize that life is not perfect or fair.
That all can't be sugar and spice, some or none, or black and white.
When we know that you take the bitter, live with the maybes
and deal with the shades of gray in between.
I will see you on the street, and you I.
You will see me for what I am, and I you.
Then we will speak, scattering the past with the dust,
and we will pass, and go our separate ways.

© 1984 Melanie White Eley

A romantic pink silk rose fastened a translucent vellum overlay to a handmade muted green colored card that was embedded with silk fibers. The raised lettering on the overlay announced:

Dr. and Mrs. Sterling G. DuBois
request the honour of your presence
at the marriage of their daughter
Elizabeth Marie
to
Steve Maximillion King

The invitation, in its fourteen karat gold stand, was positioned on top of her Chippendale dressing table as if a reminder of an event that she would otherwise forget.

"June fifteenth; that's only one week and two days away."

Sitting at the dressing table, she carefully lined her lips with a thin brush and then applied coordinating lipstick. She blotted and then read the invitation aloud. She began reading the invitation a third time but this time she stopped at the end of the first line.

"My parents, Sterling and Dorothy Dubois, have a perfect marriage that has lasted thirty-three years. Thirty-three years! That's as close to forever as you can get."

She looked at the crystal table clock next to the invitation. It was seven thirty.

"I guess I better get a move on."

She slipped on the jacket to her Prada pant suit and the matching Manolo Blahnick pumps. She stopped on her way to the back staircase to admire her size six, Vera Wang wedding dress hanging in its special place in her room sized walk-in closet. Her veil, special day underwear and wedding shoes were strategically placed on the chaise located inside the closet. Just like everything in her life, the entire wedding ensemble was perfect.

Before leaving the closet, she examined herself in the free standing, full length mirror in the corner. Using her left hand, she smoothed down a wayward strand of her straight, jet black, shoulder length hair. Then she adjusted her earrings and her watch and took one step back.

"Impeccable," she said to herself.

As she exited from her bedroom, she glanced behind to make sure she had returned everything to its proper place.

"I am so glad we decided to have hors d'oeuvre and wine passed while the photographer takes pictures. Waiting for the wedding party to arrive at the reception is so infuriating," Dorothy Dubois said as soon as Elizabeth's foot hit the bottom step of the staircase.

Her mother was standing at the sink on the other side of the counter that separated the kitchen from the family room and the keeping room. Her mother spent most of her mornings in this part of the house. Elizabeth often prayed for God to preserve her looks the way he had her mother's. Notwithstanding the graying of her temples, Dorothy looked to be the same age as Elizabeth. At fifty-five, she still wore a perfect size six just as she did the day she got pregnant with Elizabeth's older brother.

"Mother, what would we talk about if I weren't getting married?" Elizabeth asked.

"Oh, we would probably argue about something or I'd be asking you when you were going to get married. You're already thirty. I was starting to worry that you were going to grow old with your law books," her mother teased. "But seriously, I am so excited and happy that you are marrying a man who is capable of taking care of my sweet little spoiled girl in the matter to which she has grown accustomed."

Dorothy cupped Elizabeth's face in her hands and kissed her on the forehead. Elizabeth pulled away and took a piece of toast out of the toaster just as it popped up.

"Is this my breakfast," she jokingly asked her mother.

"Did you ask Debbie to fix toast for you? She put it in and then went up the front stairs. You know, sometimes I think she cleans rooms that are already clean."

"She does, Mother. I guess she doesn't want to have another encounter of the close kind with Daddy. If you notice, she is more careful about cleaning the rooms that he uses the most, like the basement. You can eat off the floor in his media room. How did she manage to make terra cotta tile shine? Don't tell her I ate her toast.

"By the way Mother," Elizabeth continued, "age only matters if you're going to have children and since I'm not, I'm good."

The clank of the porcelain bone china cup forcefully hitting its matching saucer echoed from the glass top of the breakfast table in the keeping room where her mother was now sitting.

"What?" her mother exclaimed.

An amused Elizabeth, ignoring her mother's look of indignation, responded, "Do we have to discuss the wedding this morning? I need to leave a little early."

Her mother sucked her teeth.

"We can talk about the photographer, and children, this evening."

"Oh yeah, I might be a little late," Elizabeth said right before she put the last of the toast in her mouth. Then she retrieved her matching Louis Vuitton brief case and purse from it designated place just inside the keeping room and kissed her mother on the cheek.

"Love ya, mom."

Elizabeth walked across the attached three car garage, pass her mother's Mercedes SUV, to her Lexus SC 430, an engagement gift from her parents. Even with the garage door closed, she could feel the heat and humidity. Most days, Elizabeth paid no attention to the weather. She normally drove directly into her assigned parking space in the enclosed decks below her office. Today was going to be different.

She remotely opened the garage door, started the car and then pushed the button to automatically let down the convertible roof. Laying over her head rest was a large scarf that she pulled loosely around her hair. She pulled her sunglasses from the visor and placed them on her face.

Checking her image in the rear view mirror she said, "Jacqueline Bouvier Kennedy Onassis, she was the perfect woman, as least from what I read. She is my idol. They don't make them like that anymore. I have one more thing to do before I leave."

She checked in her purse for the train ticket she

placed there after her routine beautification outing with her best friend/maid of honor, Henri, one week earlier. Every since their high school days at Woodward Academy where they met, Elizabeth and Henri had a standing semi-weekly appointment for a manicure, pedicure and brow waxing at Lila's Hands. They had tried other nail salons but fell in love with Lila's on their first visit. Lila's was the only salon with the right mix of atmosphere; sophistication, relaxation and conversation. It was not surprising that during that outing, Elizabeth, Steve and their upcoming wedding was the topic, since at that time her wedding was only two weeks away.

"Ladies, here comes the bride," Lila said as Elizabeth entered the salon. "She snagged one of Atlanta's most eligible bachelors."

Everyone in the shop smiled at Elizabeth as she walked in and took her seat at Tracey's station. Besides Lila, Tracey, Henri and Elizabeth, there were six other women in the salon: two nail technicians and four women receiving serve or in the waiting area. Elizabeth knew or was familiar with most of them. Henri, who had arrived a few minutes earlier, was already sitting at Lila's station.

She said, "Don't hate, Lila. You know she's our girl. We've got to be nice to her. Otherwise, she won't invite us to visit her in that big fat mansion that Steve's going to buy her one day."

"I'm not hating. I am just stating," Lila responded.

Quiet giggles filled the air.

"You're a beautiful girl. I know you are going to make

a beautiful bride. Where are you having the wedding?" A woman who Elizabeth recognized as one of the salon's regular clients asked.

Henri answered for Elizabeth, "She's getting married at the large white church on Cascade Road. I don't know why. It's certainly not big enough for a wedding with thirty-five, count 'em, thirty-five bridesmaids. I helped her address and mail the first two thousand invitations. Girl, it's going to be huge but just a little crowded."

"Henri, you need to stop exaggerating. You said I was hating," Lila shrieked.

"Both of you need to stop. I am having ten attendants and there are only six hundred people on the guest list. It's a fairly modest wedding," Elizabeth interjected.

"Elizabeth, ten bridesmaids and a six hundred person guest list is not modest, at least not by most folk's standards. But then again most folk's fathers don't own pain clinics, fast food restaurants and who knows what else," Lila said.

"Wait, girl," Henri said. "You forgot to mention that her mother has spent almost every waking moment for the last year planning this wedding in addition to hiring the best wedding planner in the City of Atlanta. She is having a sit down reception in that gorgeous room at the Biltmore Hotel and you'll never guess who is performing at the reception. What's her name? Gladys Knight. This is certainly not going to be a modest affair. It is going to be elegant, exquisite and impeccable. I am so pleased that I'm going to be the third most important person in the wedding."

"Henri, please. She is more excited then I am. Anyway Lila, what can I say? I am truly blessed," Elizabeth retorted.

Elizabeth like her father was finicky to a fault. Although Tracey had been her nail tech for years, Elizabeth thought it was necessary to thoroughly examine Tracey's work. She held her hands out and then pulled them close to her eyes to examine the manicure. She would thoroughly examine Tracey's work after every coat of polish, her pedicure and her brow waxing.

After a few more cheerful volleys among the women, an elderly woman who had sat quietly in the waiting area asked, "How do you love him?"

Everyone in the salon looked at the woman. Elizabeth couldn't remember seeing her before but felt a strong sense of deja vu. She brushed it off thinking that maybe the woman was one of the salon's less regular clients that she had not seen for a while.

"Are you asking me how do I love Steve?"

"Yes, how do you love him?" the woman responded.

After a long, uncomfortable moment of silence, Elizabeth said, "With all my heart."

"What does that mean?" the woman pressed.

"It means I would do anything for him."

"Anything?"

"Yes, anything?"

The woman glided towards Elizabeth. She stood in the center of the salon and was unquestionably the center of attention.

"Would you die for him?" the woman said sternly.

Elizabeth turned as far as she could without removing her hands from the nail drying machine. "I hope he wouldn't ask me to but I guess I would. I think he would also die for me."

The woman, whose dress and voice indicated that she was in her sixties, moved with the agility of a much younger woman. She floated until she was right next to Elizabeth and looked directly into her eyes as if she was trying to see Elizabeth's soul, "Well if that's the case, what do you fear?"

Elizabeth recoiled but was not to be outdone. "You mean about Steve or about my marriage?"

"Either or both. What is it that you fear?" the woman pressed again.

Elizabeth pondered the question for only a second and then responded, "I fear God and nothing else."

Tracey prevented the woman from asking another question by abruptly interjecting, "You're so lucky. I've been praying for both of us for a long time. Now I'm going to pray for myself exclusively. I think God may have given you some of what I was supposed to get."

This time the universal chuckle sounded like a sigh of relief. Elizabeth didn't stop gazing into the woman's eyes. Unlike the spectators, Elizabeth felt respite in their conversation. She feared that if the banter stopped, the strange feeling of reprieve would go away.

"Tracey you know nothing happens by luck. God is responsible for all of our blessings," Elizabeth pronounced. "Isn't that correct, mam?

The woman gently pulled Elizabeth's hands from the drying machine and held them in hers. Her touch was comforting and Elizabeth felt totally at ease although this putative stranger had shattered Elizabeth's personal space.

"Elizabeth, I hope your responses accurately reflect your feelings. Congratulations sweetheart. My prayers are with you."

The woman released Elizabeth's hands, turned to

Lila and said, "Thank you for letting me wait here. That was a very Christian thing for you to do." Then she seemed to vanish out of the door.

No one in the salon said anything until Lila answered the question that was on everyone's mind. She said, "I don't know. Today is the first day time I've seen her."

The salon was hushed while the technicians completed Henri and Elizabeth's services. Then the two of them, following their semi-weekly routine, went to a nearby Applebee's® for dinner.

When they were settled in their booth, Elizabeth leaned forward as if she was about to reveal a deep dark secret and said softly, "Henri, that lady in the shop, she seemed to know about my uneasiness. The questions that she asked were right on point. They articulate concerns that I have had for the last few weeks. Henri, is this marriage what God planned for me?"

Henri looked shocked. She took a big gulp of her apple martini. Then she sat the glass carefully on the table.

"Elizabeth, don't block your blessings."

"Henri, this is more than simple jitters."

"Elizabeth, it can't be. Steve is handsome, charismatic, smart and motivated. And he is a genuinely nice person. He's thoughtful, considerate, loyal, caring but best of all, he loves you. Actually, he worships the ground you walk on. While most single men are trying to be like the virtual thugs in the videos, God blessed you with a God fearing, professional, family man. Relax. This is a match made in heaven. You'll be fine. Don't let that woman take your joy."

"Henri, I know he loves me and I certainly love him. But sometimes love is not enough. Look at my parents. They have something special. Their relationship is ideal. I don't know what makes it that way but it's more than simple love. I don't know if we have that . . . extra."

"Listen to yourself. Elizabeth have you forgotten everything we learned in bible study. 1 Corinthians 13:13. 'And now these three remain: faith, hope and love. But the greatest of these is love.' Elizabeth, the greatest is 'love.'"

"You're right; the greatest is love but not the only. There is also faith and hope. No problem there; I have both of those. And so, Henri, what am I afraid of?"

Henri responded in a whispering yell, "Nothing. You answered the question correctly. You fear God and nothing else. It's just the jitters. Have another apple martini and then get a good night sleep. In the morning, you will have forgotten about that stupid woman and her stupid questions."

Elizabeth knew that Henri, like most of their friends, was enamored. Elizabeth wasn't quite sure if it was with Steve, the fact that he was filthy rich, the plans for an impeccable wedding or just simply the idea of marriage. Either way, Elizabeth knew they were all incapable of hearing anything against her marriage to Steve.

As Henri continued to harp on the virtues of the marriage, Elizabeth's apprehension swelled. Eventually, Elizabeth decided that, unless she could eliminate her concerns, she was not going to marry Steve. By the time she left the restaurant, she knew that sometime within the next few days, she was going to have to get away, far away, so that she could think without interference.

She thought about driving to Château Élan but she needed to go somewhere where familiarity would not obstruct with the decision she needed to make. Plus driving, even in her brand new car, was out. She had never been one for driving long distances alone and, in her current state of mind, this wasn't the time to start. A plane ride was also out. She didn't have the energy to deal with the hassle of airport security. She suddenly remembered the open train pass that her Aunt Grace, who worked for the railroad, had given her just in case Elizabeth ever wanted to experience "the real world." No date or location was specified on the ticket because "it doesn't matter where you go, Sweetie, you just need to see how the other half lives." She went home and immediately placed it in her purse.

She had been carrying the pass in her purse since that evening. Just like every morning since then, Elizabeth pulled it out and looked at it. Today was the day to use it. She returned it to the safety of the side pocket of her purse. She put the car in reverse, backed out of the garage and headed downtown. As she was driving west on I-20, she called her office.

"Department of Law, Ms. Dubois' office," her assistant said when she answered the telephone.

"Joyce, I don't have any meetings today, do I? Good. I won't be in and I may not be in tomorrow either."

"Are you Ok?"

"Yes."

There was a moment of silence while Joyce waited for an explanation. They had come to know each other well over the three years they'd worked together. Elizabeth knew that Joyce sensed that something was wrong. However, like the rest of her friends, her co-workers were ecstatic about her marriage. She felt that disclosing her concerns to Joyce would lead to another discussion about how great Steve was. She did not want to listen to anyone else try to convince her that her extreme anxiety was only pre-wedding jitters

"Really Joyce, I'm Ok. I just have a few loose ends to tie up."

"Well, Elizabeth, take care of yourself. You won't be any good to Steve or anyone else if you're not healthy in body, mind and spirit."

"Thanks, Joyce. I'll do just that."

She pulled into the lot behind the train station. Concerned about leaving her car in one spot for an indefinite period of time, she parked where it was visible from the station window and less likely to be vandalized. She opened the glove compartment and pulled out the note that she had written the same day she put the pass in her purse. She read it aloud.

Mother,

I love you. Please don't be alarmed by my absence. I will return soon. I needed to get away and gather the strength to go through with this marriage or to walk awy. I don't want to hurt you or anyone. I have got to make sure this is right for me. Tell Daddy, his little Ms. Perfect is OK.

Your daughter,
Elizabeth

"That will work."

She planned to call when she was far enough away to resist her mother's certain pleas to come home and talk. However, just in case someone recognized her car and contacted her parents before then, she laid the note open on the driver's seat. After all, a red Lexus with a vanity license plate which read "LDYLWYR" was easy to recognize.

When she entered the station, the ticket agent was sitting in the passenger waiting area. No one else was in there. Under normal circumstances the seediness of the poorly maintained station would have caused her to turn around and leave. However, these weren't normal circumstances.

She showed the agent her ticket and asked, "When is the next train leaving."

"Well there is a train boarding right now and it has open first class berths. It is going to . . . . Wait Ms.! Do you have any luggage?"

Elizabeth was already half way down the concrete stairs leading to the wooden passenger loading platform. She felt the sun on her face and realized that she still had on her Jackie ensemble. She didn't bother to remove the scarf or the glasses. Over her shoulder was the emergency bag that she kept in her car. It contained a toothbrush, toothpaste, a change of underwear and other essential toiletries. She thought she probably looked like a terrorist and was surprised no one stopped her.

Clandestinely carrying her intense anxiety for the last few weeks had been intense. She was exhausted. As soon as she was seated in the first class section of the train, she laid her head back and looked out of the window. Without warning, the world outside began moving slowly away, then faster and then faster. Eventually, focusing on the view made her dizzy. She closed her eyes.

"Hello Elizabeth. I don't think I introduced myself to you at Lila's. My name is Gabrielle."

The woman from Lila's Hands was sitting next to her. Although, she was trying to get away from anything or anyone familiar with her or her marriage, Elizabeth's instinct told her Gabrielle could help her find out why she was so apprehensive. She was actually grateful Gabrielle was there.

"Hello, Ms. Gabrielle. How did you get into my berth? Where are you headed?" Elizabeth said as she sat up and adjusted her clothes.

"I guess I'm going where you're going since we're on the same train."

Elizabeth giggled nervously and said, "You know, I'm really not sure where I'm going. I didn't listen when the agent attempted to tell me. Where are we?"

"Instead of riding this train to you-don't-know-where, why aren't you home planning your wedding?"

"I don't know, Ms. Gabrielle. For the last few weeks I've felt a little off base. I couldn't articulate what was brothering me until we talked last week at the salon. Why were you there anyway? You didn't get any services."

"Please don't call me Ms. Gabrielle. It reminds me of exactly how old I really am. Gabrielle is fine."

"Why did you ask those questions?"

"I wanted you to think. Do you really love Steve or are those just words; nothing more than a noisy gong or a clanging cymbal?"

"You just quoted 1 Corinthians, the love chapter from the bible. That verse stands for the ultimate importance of love in our lives. Yes, I love Steve and I have no doubt he loves me. Ms. Gabrielle, you tell me, why am I afraid."

"There you go with that 'Ms.' again. Did you answer that question honestly at the salon?"

"Well, I do fear God. In fact right now, I'm afraid that God wants me to do something other than marry Steve."

"That's not correct. God wants you to get married but only if you truly comprehend the commitment necessary to have a lasting marriage. God wishes everyone would understand the marriage commitment."

"Why isn't our love enough?"

"Why are you afraid?"

"I don't know. Why do you keep asking me that? Why don't you answer the questions that I asked?" Elizabeth said. She folded her arms across her chest and sucked her teeth.

Gabrielle continued to press Elizabeth, "Would you die for him?"

Elizabeth snapped back, "Ms. Gabrielle, we're too young to think about dying. We're just beginning our lives together."

"Too young? Elizabeth, babies die before they are born. Ok, let me put it another way. What if you wake up the day after the wedding and nothing is like you thought it would be? What if, at the beginning, you think your life and marriage is perfect. Then later you discover that it is not? Are you committed to the marriage and resolving the issues that are guaranteed to arise?"

Elizabeth pondered the question, and then responded meekly, "I don't know. Why do you think we're going to have problems?"

"1 Corinthian 13 is about perfect, unconditional love. God wants everyone to strive for perfection although God is the only one that achieves it. Loving unconditionally means you make a conscious commitment to love an imperfect person, in an imperfect relationship. Are you afraid to make that choice, Elizabeth?"

This time Elizabeth didn't answer. Gabrielle leaned forward in her seat and took hold of Elizabeth hands; her touch calmed the exasperation rising in Elizabeth.

"Elizabeth, not all of your dreams will be realized. Nor will all of your expectations be met. The people in your life and circumstances of your life will change; sometimes for the better and sometimes for the worst. That's life and that's marriage. Marriages that last – the ones that survive despite the imperfections - are based on unconditional love."

"Unconditional love?" Elizabeth said as if she had never heard the phrase before.

"Yes, love that can not be destroyed by life."

"Ms. Gabrielle, would I be committed to love an adulterous, abusive husband who didn't love me?"

"No but sometimes unconditional love can even turn those situations around. However, it would be an unsound relationship if you were made to choose between the respect which is a major component of unconditional love for yourself and love of someone else. That would be an unsound relationship. Staying in a perpetually unsound relationship, would mean you have confused obsession with unconditional love. God does not condone a flawed relationship."

"But Ms, Gabrielle, God forbid, what if he turns out to be a child molester or murderer? Would I still love him?"

"You probably would even if you didn't want to. However, unconditional love doesn't mean that you would support and be loyal to him while he committed sins against God or society. No, it means you do whatever necessary to save him and his soul; even if you had to report him to the officials or leave him. He may hate you and you may suffer. Unconditional love is not a shield from pain.

"Molestation and murder are the extremes. A more likely scenario is, at age fifty, you realize you've reached the half point in your life without realizing your dreams. Will you hate him for not fighting harder for your dreams or for that matter, his own dreams? Will you resent the children that you had for him because of the inevitable impetus that they will have played on the direction of your life? Or will you be thankful that wherever you are at that time, you two have arrived there together?"

"Are you saying that if I love Steve unconditionally, my marriage still won't be perfect but it will last? I just don't understand why I can't have a perfect and lasting marriage like my parents?"

"Elizabeth, what do you fear?"

"I'm afraid that you are asking the right questions but all of my answers are wrong." Elizabeth squeezed Gabrielle hands tighter.

Gabrielle smiled and moved her head slowly from side to side. "There are no wrong answers; just open and honest ones. What is wrong is you're not discussing this with those who love you unconditionally. They won't judge you. They'll help you to resolve your issues. Go home, Elizabeth. You need to talk to your parents and Steve."

"Thank you, Ms. Gabrielle. You're a saint."

"I'd rather be called 'Saint' than 'Ms.'"

Elizabeth laughed and looked out of the window. When she turned back, Gabrielle was gone. Just then the engineer announced that the train would be leaving in ten minutes. Elizabeth realized she was still in Atlanta. She jumped up and ran until she reached her car. Before she sat down, she picked up the emergency note. It was in her hand when she entered the house.

"Mother, where are you?" she squealed.

Dorothy was still in the keeping room admiring

her rose garden. She was just finishing her second cup of morning tea.

"Elizabeth, I'm right here. What's the matter?"

Elizabeth handed her mother the note and stood silently as Dorothy read it. Dorothy looked up from the note, examined Elizabeth's face and then read the note again.

"What is this about, Elizabeth? Are you going somewhere?"

"No, I already went. Well I tried to go but I met this woman. Well, I think I met this woman . . . ,"

Dorothy walked over to Elizabeth and tenderly rubbed her hand across her daughter's cheek. She directed Elizabeth to the plush overstuffed micro fiber chair located in the corner of the keeping room. After she was seated, Dorothy removed Elizabeth's shoes and placed her feet on the matching ottoman.

"Elizabeth, calm down. I'll fix you a cup of tea while you gather your thoughts. Would you prefer green tea or Tazo Chai Latte?"

"Whatever you are having will be fine."

Elizabeth sat quietly, watching her mother's movement in the kitchen. How was she going to tell her mother about her conversation with Gabrielle without sounding like a lunatic? When Dorothy returned with the tea she sat on the Ottoman directly in front of Elizabeth. She lifted Elizabeth's feet into her lap and began to massage them.

"Mother, I met a woman named . . . ."

"Gabrielle," her mother completed the sentence. "Actually, you were visited by your guardian angel, Gabrielle."

"Gabrielle, of course," Elizabeth said hitting herself gently on the forehead. "But how did you know?"

Unconditional

"People born on the same day of the week share a guardian angel. We were both born on Monday. Therefore, we share Gabrielle. I'm sure you've met her before now. You just don't remember."

"That's probably why she seemed so familiar. She told me to come home and talk to you."

"I knew she would visit you right before your wedding, just like she did me."

"What? Why did she visit you?"

"I was having second thoughts about my marriage, just like you are having now. She tried to help me understand why."

"I didn't know you knew. Why didn't you say something?"

"I'm your mother. You can't hide much from me. However, as hard as it may be for me, I have to let you deal with your problems in your own way and on your own schedule. It would be great if you could learn from my experiences but unfortunately it doesn't work that way."

"Were you afraid? Or as Saint Gabrielle says, 'What did you fear?'"

Her mother smiled, "Yes, I was afraid."

"Of what? Mother, you and Daddy are perfect together. "

"Perfect! Your Dad and I! What makes you think that?"

"He treats you like you're God's gift to the world. Now that I think about it, you treat him the same way."

"Doesn't Steve treat you good?"

"Yes, but we don't seem to be on the same wave length like you and Dad. You like the same things. You do the same things. Mother, you are so intertwined that you finish each other's sentences. Even when you don't agree, you can manage to agree to disagree."

"Elizabeth! We are God's gift to each other but our relationship is far from perfect. It took us a lifetime to get here. Even with that, it is still an imperfect relationship between two imperfect people that is blessed with mutual unconditional love."

"Did Gabrielle tell you to say that?"

"No," her mother responded with a laugh. "But I'm sure she said something similar to you.

"Elizabeth, our relationship is our relationship. Yours won't be like ours because, even though people say we are alike, you are not me and Steve is not your Dad. I hope you are not gauging your relationship against ours. I hope you reach a point in your marriage where you are content and comfortable like we are, but I certainly hope your road to that point will not be as rocky as mine has been."

"Rocky? Are you talking about helping Daddy start his practice? I know that was hard on you but I wouldn't call it rocky. Anyway look at the results. You have everything any woman could want: a big house, a nice car, minks, and diamonds."

"Elizabeth! Those are material things. They can't make you happy nor will they make your marriage last. Do you remember how you got that small scar over your eye?"

"Do you mean this one?" Elizabeth pointed at a barely visible half inch scar just above her right eyelid. "I thought it was a birth mark."

"No, I wish it was that simple." Her mother took a deep breath and picked her tea cup from the end table. She took a sip and exaggerated swallowing. Then resumed massaging Elizabeth's feet and said, "Let me explain how you got it.

"When your Dad and I got married I, of course, was much younger. I was also very insecure. I was afraid that your father didn't love me enough."

"You mean you were afraid he didn't love you unconditionally," Elizabeth said mockingly.

"Exactly. You have been listening to Gabrielle," her mother noted and then continued, "I was afraid that once he realized who I really was, he would leave me. I don't know why I thought he didn't know that before we got married. We dated for a year and were engaged for another. After my discussion with Gabrielle, I decided that my love was strong enough to sustain a marriage. I'm sure that wasn't what she wanted me to glean from the conversation."

"I don't think that's the message she is trying to give me either," Elizabeth sighed.

"Sometimes I wonder why God gave us personal choice," her mother replied jokingly. "Anyway, after the wedding, my doubts consumed me. Believe it or not, Elizabeth, I got pregnant immediately because I knew your father would love his first child unconditionally. I prayed that love would tie him to me."

"Mother! No! You always told me that having a child to hold on to a man is wrong and that it wouldn't work."

"It is wrong and it doesn't work."

"So?"

"My intentions were wrong and it didn't work. Your father didn't stay with me because he loved your brother. He stayed because he loved me. I just didn't know it then."

"When did you finally figure that out?"

Dorothy smiled and motioned to Elizabeth to be patient. Then she continued, "The burden of trying to hold on to a man that I thought would stop loving me soon was too much for me to carry. I shut down.

"For three years, I lived in a fog. Everyday, I struggled to get out of bed. It took great efforts to make it through the day pretending to be a happy little home maker. Hiding my feelings was exhausting."

"Tell me about it," Elizabeth inserted.

Dorothy smiled again.

"Several times during that period, I yearned for a way out. I even thought about suicide. Gabrielle tried to get me to talk with her or God about my problems. But I was not in a place where I could do that.

"Then one day, as I was going through the motions, you and your brother were having a tiff, just as all siblings do. I didn't even notice that your brother had picked up a catsup bottle until I saw the blood gushing from that spot were you now have a scar. Both you and your brother start screaming. Because I was so irrational, I start screaming too. You both grabbed my legs and said, 'Mommy, we're going to make it alright.' Your brother took off his shirt and wiped the blood from your face.

"I don't remember what happened after that. Several hours later, I found myself sitting in the floor crying with the two of you asleep in my lap. The bloody stained shirt was still in your brother's hand. The fear of all of the things that could have happened overcame me. At that moment, I decided I had to get myself out of that horrible state. With time, and counseling, I resolved my issues and here I am, thirty years later, with my beautiful daughter."

"But mother, I don't remember any of that? Have we ever discussed it before?"

"I'm glad you don't remember. That was a long time ago. Maybe you forgot or maybe you blocked it out. It was such a horrible experience. We never discussed it before because I never thought we needed to. But I think it is important for you to hear it now, especially if you truly think my life is perfect.

"Let me tell you another story."

Elizabeth showed her mother the palm of her hand and said, "I've heard enough for today."

"Ok, Sweetie, no more stories. But Elizabeth I need you to understand that you are not seeing perfection. You are seeing the results of blood, sweat and tears . . . and commitment. My life has never been perfect."

"I'm beginning to understand that. Why didn't Daddy notice that you were so unhappy?"

"He did. But he silently prayed for my sadness to go away. He didn't discuss it with me because he was afraid I would tell him that I didn't love him. He had no idea that my sadness was the result of my being afraid that he didn't love me. Thank God, we've matured considerably since then."

"But why did you stay with him if you didn't think he loved you?

"Because I loved you and your brother unconditionally; I thought that was the best thing for the two of you."

"Wow. Talk about a commitment. How can I make sure my man is as committed to me as my Mother?" Elizabeth said only half kidding and hoping to bring levity to the intense conversation.

"Elizabeth, I spent years trying to make sure your father loved me unconditionally and waiting for him to show me that he didn't. Eventually, I realized that I can't make anyone, not even your father, love me. Who, how and when you are loved is not your choice. On the other hand, you can choose whether or not you will love and if that love will be unconditional. I decided to love your father unconditionally. That's what I had to contribute to make this marriage last.

"But before I could do that, first I had to decide to love God unconditionally. Then I had to learn to love myself unconditionally. Elizabeth, if you do those three things, everything else will fall in place."

Dorothy took the cups into the kitchen. Elizabeth walked in behind her. "Mother, why did you stop doing the feet thing?"

Dorothy giggled. "I was coming back."

"Mother, are you telling me that I can decide to love unconditional?"

"Well, Elizabeth, I don't think you can go from zero to sixty miles an hour without some sort of spark. But if you love him, and you say you do, you have to decide if you want to allow that love to be pervasive enough to carry you through this marriage. If you can not or are not willing to give it your all, then it would be a sin to go through with this marriage."

"Mother, we've spent thousands on the wedding and have invited people from all over the world. I can't believe that you would suggest that I call it off."

"What I am suggesting is that you do the right thing for you and Steve. He is a great guy and will make a wonderful husband. He is just the kind of man that I prayed you would find. Whether my doubts about your father's love for me were real or imaginary, I can't in good conscious suggest that you put him through the torment I went through."

"If he is such a great guy, why don't I know if I love him unconditionally?"

Dorothy hugged Elizabeth tightly. "Because you may have chosen not to know or not to love unconditionally."

"Why would I do that?"

"There could be any number of reasons. You'll find out when you determine what you fear, Elizabeth?"

Elizabeth's looked at her mother again and then walked upstairs to her bedroom, grabbing her shoes and purse on the way.

She walked through her bedroom into her personal bathroom. When she leaned over the porcelain sink and turned the brass knob, she noticed her three carat platinum engagement ring laying on the edge of the sink. She jerked her hand out in front of her face. She couldn't believe her finger had been naked all day and she hadn't even noticed that her ring was missing.

Did she leave it there intentionally? Was that a Freudian slip? Or did she just make a simple human mistake? She picked the ring up, examined it closely and then slipped it on her finger.

"Elizabeth," her mother called from her bedroom door. "Are you OK?"

"Mother, is anyone other than God perfect?" Elizabeth walked into the bedroom and sat in one of the two wing chairs in the seating area formed by the bay window.

"No," her mother said as she sat in the other.

They sat quietly as the mid-day sun filled the bay. Then Elizabeth said, "Mother, I never really wanted a big wedding."

"What?"

"I didn't want a big wedding?"

"Why didn't you say something before now?"

"At first, I got caught up in the excitement. By the time I realized what was happening, we had gone too far to turn around. Plus, I didn't think you would accept my eloping or having a small quaint ceremony in your rose garden. I guess I didn't want to disappoint you."

"Elizabeth, this isn't about me. You can't spend your life trying to be like me or trying to please me. This is your life and wedding. "

"Mother, please! You know as well as I do that this is your wedding just like the ceremony where you and Daddy got married was Grandma's wedding."

Dorothy smiled and said, "I see your point about the wedding but I hope you hear me about your life."

"But you know, I'm OK with it; the wedding that is. These are the sacrifices you have to make when you love someone unconditionally like I do you, Mother." Dorothy smiled at her daughter who was looking out of the bay window. Elizabeth continued to avoid her Mother's gaze. "By the way, we're having two."

"What?"

"If it's God's will, we're having two children. On second thought, I'm going to talk with Steve about having three," Elizabeth smiled at her mother. "But we're not going to start until after our third wedding anniversary."

. . .for better or for worse . . . until death do us part

                                        Traditional wedding vow

Setting a Screen

Dissolving pain medication in pear applesauce,
to slowly feed to you from a spoon,
felt as natural to me at thirty seven, as I'm sure,
cutting a peanut butter and jelly sandwich in triangles,
to feed me at eight, felt to you.
Thank you for not cutting the bread all the way through,
giving me a perforation that I could slowly pull apart.
My daughter now likes hers cut the same way.

Struggling to lift your six foot four inch self off of the floor,
when your once track-running limbs betrayed you,
finally failed you;
made me as anxious at thirty seven, as I'm sure,
trying to change my diaper on your lap,
but only succeeding in rolling my five month self onto the floor,
made you.
Thank you for putting my mind at ease with your laughter, both times.

Realizing that you, who was adored and sought out by many,
chose me, to entrust your whole true self to;
felt as incredible to me, as I'm sure,
knowing you had my complete acceptance of your same gender love,
must have felt to you.
Thank you for showing me the pinnacle of courage.

The nurturing and comfort of a grandmother's hands.
The guiding resilience in a father's voice.
The example of faith and strength of a dear childhood friend.
Thank you all for your parting gifts.

I received them well.

©2005 Melanie White Eley

JOURNAL

Saturday, August 27, 2005, 10:30 PM

Today, at the request of the Governor of Louisiana, President Bush declared a state of emergency. Mayor Nagin told everyone to leave New Orleans. His exact words were:

> Board up your homes, make sure you have enough medicine, make sure the car has enough gas. Do all the things you normally do for a hurricane but treat this one differently because it is pointed towards New Orleans.

The officials at Tulane University suspended classes. The odds that Hurricane Katrina will hit the city are pretty high. When she struck Miami the other day she was a category one. She did a little damage and dropped a lot of rain. Then she went back into the ocean. Now she's swirling in the gulf, getting stronger by the minute. They're predicting that she'll hit New Orleans as a category four or five. I'm not sure what that means but I know the wind speed and water surge will be ferocious.

That is if she hits at all. That's just a prediction. Nobody knows if, where or when Katrina will land. The news reports say that the Mayor is thinking about issuing a mandatory evacuation order. Why didn't he do it today if the storm is going to be so bad? Last month the president of one of the parishes issued a mandatory evacuation order, and nothing happened at all. In fact, this is the fourth time we've been told to evacuate in the last three months. I didn't leave before and I'm not leaving now.

Of course, I should leave. I'm actually afraid to stay. I ought to be. Hurricane Camille ripped my parents and brother out of our house. Their bodies were never recovered. Between that and the natural order of things, the only members of my family left are a few cousins that I rarely talk to now. I wish we were closer. We used to be. I don't know what happened. It seems like when Grandma died, the family died. What I really wish is that Grandma could have lived forever.

Now that's why Dr. Barbou told me to write in this journal. It helps me focus on my feelings. I think I'm even getting a handle on my fears and my guilt. It's only taken me thirty-six years to almost believe that it's not my fault that I survived. I'm going to stay, ride out this hurricane, and face my fear right here in my one hundred and twenty-five year old Victorian house. I need to stay here and protect it. This is my home now that Grandma's house is no longer in the family.

But that's not the only reason I'm staying. When I was a student in Tulane's law school (that seems so long ago) every time there was a hurricane warning, we'd have a hurricane party. I'd get with some friends, go to Baton Rouge or Houston, rent a hotel room, and drink and party until the storm passed. Then we'd go back to school hung over and behind in all of our classes. Almost every time, New Orleans would be spared or there would be little or no damage. I really must have been a sick puppy; first for having a hurricane party and then for being too stupid to have it where the hurricane was suppose to hit. On second thought, maybe that wasn't so stupid after all.

Unconditional

Now that I'm back in New Orleans, I'm not going to fall into that same pattern. I don't have time for that nonsense anymore. I have too much going on. I've got to teach and prepare for classes. They're going to resume on the first of September. I have to be back the day before, whether or not I go to a hurricane party. We're supposed to finish grading the bar examines next week. I'm staying right here.

I'm so glad Raymond understands. Sometimes talking to that man is like pulling teeth. We finally got our plans straight. I'm going to spend winter break with him in Tallahassee. Then when I leave, he will have about a week to prepare for his deployment. When he returns from Germany, I'll be finishing up the spring semester, and he'll spend the summer with me here in New Orleans. He'll be going back to active duty just before fall semester begins.

I still don't quite understand why he doesn't want to get married while he is on active duty, but he's my man. I have to respect him, and his wishes. Finally, after seven years, I can see the light at the end of the tunnel; just one more year. I just know he's going to propose when I see him at Christmas. Maybe we can plan the wedding during the summer. I'm getting pregnant as soon as we get married. I'll be forty soon. My biological clock is about to stop ticking. Waiting for Raymond, I almost missed the opportunity to have a child. Funny, they're calling the storm Katrina. That was one of the names I was considering for my little girl.

Feeling for the day: determination and anxiety.

Nycki Whiting

Sunday, August 28, 2005, 10:00 PM

This morning the Mayor made the evacuation order mandatory. Ten thousand people have already gone to the Superdome, which has been designated as the shelter of last resort. The Mayor advised them to eat well before they came and to bring enough rations to last at least three days. The Red Cross has opened other temporary shelters, and is prepared to follow the storm into the area. The ports are closed, and there is a six o'clock curfew for anyone staying in the city.

I went on the internet to see if I could get a better understanding of the kind of damage a category five hurricane would do to the city. It didn't take me long to find the National Weather Services' Web page that forecasted that the storm will cause the city to be uninhabitable for weeks. The walls and roofs of smaller buildings will blow away, and windows of hurricane resistant high rise buildings will be shattered. The wind will make cars and trucks airborne, and of course, there will be extensive power outages.

When I read that simple exposure to the wind could kill, I was convinced that I needed to leave. If that wasn't terrifying enough, there were indications that the levees, built for a category three storm, were likely to break under the impact of Katrina. I packed a few things in an overnight bag, grabbed some blankets and pillows, and called James at home and on his cell. All the circuits were busy; I couldn't reach him.

Most of my other friends have already left. Some went home or somewhere or anywhere except the gulf coast. Quite a number of them went to Baton Rouge to you-know-whose house. Not even a hurricane could make me go there. Although he wanted to go at the first mention of Katrina, I knew James hadn't left. I told him to go if he felt that was best but he refused to leave without me. He has been trying to convince me that we should "exit stage coach right" immediately. (Yes, he's a little corny.) He keeps telling me about what happened when Hurricane Pam hit New Orleans. I never heard of Hurricane Pam. I don't know who paired us as Morehouse brother and Spelman sister, but they did a good job. James has been my best friend since we met on the first day of undergrad; (my best male friend that is. I don't think I'll ever have another best female friend.) He knows me better than anyone else in the world, including Raymond.

But sometimes I wonder about my buddy James. He's been in New Orleans the same amount of time that I have: three years for law school and two years as a college professor with an eleven year break in between. Somehow he learned the art of being a voodoo priest. I don't know when he could have studied without me knowing. We are together almost all of the time. If he's not a priest, I sure would like to know where he learned how to see the future. Truth is it doesn't matter because I love him and I respect his premonitions. Most times, I heed his warning without discussion. The Katrina stubbornness was definitely an exception; probably brought on by too much psychotherapy.

Before I could contact him this morning, James knocked on my door. At first, he had fear on his face but it turned to relief when he saw my bag. Since he knew that I would not agree to go to you-know-whose house, his mother helped him make arrangements for us to stay with a Ms. Roulette in Baton Rouge. His mother wanted him to come home to Atlanta but since we were leaving so late, they didn't think it was a good idea for us to be on the road. Once Katrina lands she will weaken, but she'll still be a pretty powerful storm.

I had a full tank of gas; so I drove. Even though the state officials had arranged for all lanes on the freeway and streets to lead out of New Orleans, the heavy traffic turned a one hour ride into a three hour creep. During the entire ride, James was surfing the radio listening to different versions of the news. They were all estimating that at least one hundred thousand people would remain in the city. When I joked that I should have been one of them, James responded in a dismal tone that a lot of those people were going to die. I wanted him to be wrong, but I was pretty sure he was right. That was when I truly comprehended the probable gravity of the catastrophe that was about to happen and, but for the grace of God and my last minute serge of good sense, we both would have been smack damn in the middle of it.

My parents also decided not to evacuate when Camille was approaching Biloxi. My father didn't want to go to the shelter at our segregated church. He was afraid that we would be trapped and the officials wouldn't even look for us until the white folks needed their houses cleaned. When the sirens sounded, warning us that the storm was near, Momma told me and Little Man to come into the hall closet with her and Daddy. Instead, I ran into the basement to be with Grandma. My father was searching for me when the storm hit.

A few days later, the clean-up crew found my parents' wedding rings down the road tied together with a shoe string. They never found anything of my bother. Everybody in our neighborhood knew about my parent's strange habit of tying their meager gold bands together at the threat of a hurricane. They said that was a message to God that even in death, they wanted to be together. They also said that it was to remind us that even after they are gone, my brother and I needed to remain united as a family. I suddenly realized that I had put James, the closest thing I have to a brother, at risk of suffering the same fate as my family.

I pulled over to the shoulder of the road. I told James that I needed to rest for a minute, but I know he sensed that something else was wrong. Without saying a word, he pulled me out of the car and close to him. He wrapped his arms tightly around me and I felt like nothing, not even Katrina could harm either of us. (He's so good at calming me down. He should be. He's had plenty of practice.) Eventually my anxiety subsided, and we got back in the car. James took over the driving and we listened to my favorite CD for the rest of the ride. Later he asked if I felt better. I told him I was alright and that I had been overwhelmed by the people who could die in the storm.

When we found the house, James said maybe we should go somewhere else; somewhere with people we know. I knew where he meant but I wasn't going. I responded there wasn't anywhere else to go. Then, just before he rung the doorbell, I told him that we could leave as soon as it was safe to return to New Orleans. He chuckled before he said that God smiles whenever you say tomorrow. (Sometimes he's too deep for me.)

Ms. Roulette, a small fair skinned Cajun woman with long, jet black hair, opened the door. She starred at us for a long time. When she finally let us in, she immediately directed us to our room. It was obvious that she didn't want us sitting in the living room with her. Later, when James called his mother to tell her that we were out of New Orleans, we learned that Ms. Roulette was a friend of a friend of a friend and she had to be convinced to take in some "New Orleans scum."

She has three bedrooms in addition to hers but she is making James and I share a room. Maybe she thinks we are a couple or maybe she doesn't want to have to disinfect her whole house after we leave. At any rate, we don't mind. Just like always, James is lying across the bed and I'm laying the long way with my feet in the small of his back. This used to be our favorite way to study.

Since the room doesn't have a radio or a television, every so often one of us ventures out to get an update on Katrina. She is still moving slowly up the gulf. It appears that she may be veering to the east and away from a direct hit on New Orleans. I wonder if there is any chance that she will dissipate before she hits land. That's what I'm praying for her to do.

I called Raymond just a few minutes ago but he was in a hurry. He said he might be able to call me back tonight. Cell phone transmissions are jammed but I put my phone by my side just in case. I'm glad I'm with James. I don't know how I would have made it today otherwise.

Feeling for the day: enhanced judgment.

Monday, August 29, 2005, 7:30 PM

I'm drained tonight. It has been a long two days. I'm not sure if Ms. Roulette even went to bed last night. She was sitting in her reclining chair, looking at television when we went to bed and when we woke up this morning. She reluctantly permitted us to sit in the living room with her. We spent the day watching Katrina news.

It seems like New Orleans braced for extreme damages that didn't occur. The storm did hit New Orleans though. It ripped two holes in the roof of the Superdome and now it's raining on the unfortunate people who went there to wait out the storm. There are reports of flooding in St. Bernard Parish but no one knows to what extent. Some windows were blown out of some buildings. Other than a few fallen shutters and a lot of rain, the French Quarter and downtown New Orleans are still in tack. I wonder if our houses were damaged.

Ground zero for Katrina was Mississippi. She desecrated a number of cities including Biloxi. She also did some damage to areas along the coast in Alabama. It's amazing to actually see how wind can pick up buildings and cars and set them down miles away. There's a casino sitting in the middle of US 90. Utility poles are leaning over like the Tower of Pisa. Trees were pulled up by their roots; some broke in half like tooth picks. Entire neighborhoods look like King Kong walked on them and flattened them to the ground. The weather service's forecast was correct, but the prediction about where Katrina would land was incorrect.

I've experienced many hurricanes in my life. None of them have caught my interest like Katrina. Certainly being an evacuee (what a title) from New Orleans is the main reason. Maybe my interest is also peaked because of Katrina's similarity to Camille. Seeing the damage on television has given me a better grasp of how destructive a category five hurricane can be. It certainly reinforces my belief in a higher power. Even if I had stayed in New Orleans, there would have been nothing I could have done to protect my house. Just like at three, I had no control over Camille or her impact. Grandma told me that a million times, but my hardhead didn't listen.

Ms. Roulette was disappointed that the city had been spared. She referred to New Orleans as a human landfill. She said that most people who visit New Orleans never venture past the French Quarter, downtown, and the convention center. They never see the part where those poor black people live. She went on to say that those areas are worst than ghettos, and the world would be better without them. I wasn't sure if the "them" was the people, the public housing projects or both.

A few days ago a colleague also advocated the elimination of the New Orleans. He felt that God would smash the hurricane into the city to rid it of the pervasive sin for which it is known. That rationale is so flawed. Sin is everywhere in the world. If God was going to use natural disasters to eliminate sin, then the entire world would simply explode. I'm certain God has the power to do that, if he chooses to do so, but he doesn't. God gave man free will. When we use that free will to sin, unless we repent, we spend eternity in hell. That's God's punishment for our sin; not being destroyed by a hurricane.

Still I hoped that Ms. Roulette's reason for wanting the destruction of the city was because of its sinful reputation. Surely she was compassionate enough to understand that no matter how dilapidated, those projects are home to some people. I'd much rather be around someone whose flawed rationale is based in Christianity, than with someone so insensitive. Or worst yet, someone whose flawed rationale is based in hate.

As it turns out, her hate is based in Christianity. As least she thinks she's a Christian, as do other like-minded people. In her opinion, God should have removed the projects because the Government couldn't figure out how to get rid of "them." She went on to say that God would be doing everyone a favor, even those underprivileged folks who, no matter where they would have lived after the storm destroyed their homes, they would be better off than they are now.

The conversation made me ill. How could anybody be so stupid? When I was younger, living with my grandmother, we were poor as a church mouse, as Grandma used to say. I never realized that was a "problem" until I became a relatively well paid law school professor. Then I saw how people equate race with poverty, and then use poverty as a reason to be racist. However, that realization didn't change my feelings. Neither did the amount of money that I made. That two-bedroom, white clapper board, shot gun house in rural Biloxi was and will always be home to me.

I wanted to tell her that maybe next time God would rid the world of all racist half-breeds like her. Of course, I don't believe that. Although I don't know why He would send such a destructive hurricane, God certainly wouldn't have created Katrina to rid New Orleans of African-Americans, or any specific group of people. My guess, and I think it's a good one, is that God is color blind. I wanted to tell her that too, but instead I sat quietly, watching the news, rocking back and forth in my chair, feeling like an unwanted guest.

A little while later, James convinced me to come to bed. So here I am writing in my journal at seven-thirty in the evening. He makes me sick when he acts like my father. As soon as I heard that New Orleans was spared, I wanted to leave. He refused. Maybe he's right; it isn't a good idea to go back into the city with the heavy rains lagging behind Katrina. Plus, we really need to give the officials time to assess the full extent of the damage. Actually this afternoon there were reports of more flooding, but those reports weren't confirmed. We're leaving first thing in the morning, regardless.

I haven't talked with Raymond today. I tried to call him earlier, but he didn't answer his phone. I'm sure the cell towers are down. That's why he hasn't checked on me. I'll try calling him in the morning.

Feeling for the day: disgust and loathing.

Tuesday August 30, 2005, 5:30 PM

I don't know where to begin. It seems so trivial to talk about what I did today, or how I feel. New Orleans is filling up like a saucer under a faucet. Wait, I'm getting ahead of myself. I can't reach my counselor, but I know she would tell me to work through my feelings systematically. That's real important today since, other than horror and shock, I have no idea what I'm feeling.

James and I woke up about five-thirty this morning, and prepared to leave for New Orleans. Even though I didn't want to, I wrote a note thanking Ms. Roulette for her hospitality. (I know Grandma looked down on me and smiled. She raised me right.) We tiptoed to the front door. Ms. Roulette was asleep in her reclining chair. The television was on but James wouldn't let me watch.

When we got in the car, I turned to the twenty-four hour news station. It was then that we learned of Katrina's cruel trick. She spared New Orleans, but spewed one hundred and forty-five mile an hour winds and a twenty-foot water surge into Lake Pontchartrain, desecrating the already weaken levees. The floodwall broke in two places and water was flowing into the Ninth Ward where the poor people live. There were thousands of people standing on their roofs waiting to be rescued. The Army Corp of Engineers was dropping sand bags in the break, but they were disappearing in the rushing water. Within a twenty-four hour period, New Orleans has been hit by two disasters.

When I was in law school, I heard that New Orleans was below sea level. I never really understood how a city could be ten feet below the level of the sea or how important the levees were to the city. I asked James if the water flowing into the city would rise ten feet and wouldn't that cover some of the small houses in New Orleans. He told me not to worry; the officials had been planning this eventuality for years. That was the benefit of Hurricane Pam. He explained that Hurricane Pam was a simulation that the officials had created to see the impact of such a fierce storm on New Orleans and the levees. He had read the report and knew that it was detailed right down to how people without vehicles would have to be taken to safety. (His BS in civil engineering and photographic memory comes in handy sometimes.)

I felt better when James told me that the first response workers were probably waiting for the storm to pass. They'll be in the impacted areas to save the stranded people soon. But, of course, this was no time for us to go back to the city. We were going to have to stay with Ms. Roulette a little while longer; at least until we could decide where we were going to go until the city was restored. However, the thought of going back into her house disgusted both of us. We decided to get breakfast first.

We eventually found a restaurant with a television that wasn't packed with people. News reporter's movement was limited and, therefore, the news was incomplete and sporadic. However, it was clear that the situation all along the gulf coast was bleak. Water was still flowing into the New Orleans. Several major roadways, including Interstate Ten, had been washed out. Oil refineries located alone the gulf coast had been damaged by the wind or drowned by the flood and Katrina wasn't finished. She was causing havoc as she traveled north spinning off tornados and dumping large amounts of rain as she passed.

Even with these gloomy circumstances, neither of us wanted to go back to Ms. Roulette's. There were "no vacancy" signs on every hotel we passed. When I told James we were blessed to even have somewhere to stay, he responded that we actually had two places: Ms. Roulette's and you-know-whose. He said that he preferred you-know-whose, and they would be elated if both of us came. I pondered that choice for just a moment. No matter how uncomfortable, you-know-whose would be better than staying with a self-hating curmudgeon. At least, our friends would be there, and we wouldn't be on self-imposed exile in a stranger's guest bedroom. I knew he wouldn't go without me, and after what I almost did to James, I owed him this.

As soon as I said alright, we headed to the house where my ex-fiancé lived with his wife, my ex-best girl friend. I hadn't spoken to either of them since our first year of law school, when they confessed that they had unintentionally fallen in love and wanted to date. When I accepted the professorship at Tulane, I didn't know he was the dean of the law school at Southern University, and she was an attorney for the State of Louisiana. Consequently, we all run in the same circles, and I spend a lot of time avoiding them. However, in the wake of the worst storm to hit the country since Camille, I was coming for a visit.

As James parked the car, I begin to reconsider my decision. I was just about to tell him to take me back to Ms. Roulette's when my two ex's, accompanied by at least twenty of our friends, literally pulled us from the car, hugging us and saying how glad they were that we were safe. When we got into the house my ex's pulled me aside and assured me that I was welcome to stay as long as necessary. They pleaded with me to forgive them. They also said they had always hoped we could rebuild our relationship.

Then they ushered me into the kitchen where someone

had cooked enough fried chicken, gumbo, and sweet ice tea to feed an army. The smell of the homemade sweet potato pie sitting on the counter was intoxicating. I always tell my uppity friends that I only eat healthy foods, and most of the time that's true. However, when I used to go home to Grandma's, walk in that house and smell those pork laden collard greens, sugared ham, and homemade sweet potato pies, I'd forget how to spell cholesterol. I think I forgot how to spell it again this afternoon.

Since they heeded the voluntary evacuation, most of our friends staying with the ex's had already made arrangements. James called his mother to tell her he would be home in a few days. She's expecting him to bring me. I wouldn't mind staying with James' family. His mother treats me like her daughter. However, I don't like her always insinuating that James and I are eventually going to end up as a couple. Why would I give up such a great friendship for sex? I have Raymond for that.

I think I want to go to Tallahassee to be with Raymond. My cousin called and told me to come to her house. After we graduated from Spelman, she married a Morehouse man and they stayed in Atlanta. It might be nice to be with her but I don't know if I want to go there. It certainly won't be the same without Grandma.

I miss Grandma so much. I talk to her often. I certainly could use one of her hugs. When I was younger, I had dreams that made me wake up screaming. The nightmares weren't always the same, but they always ended with Grandma dying. She would sit on the edge of my bed, hug me tight and whisper in my ear "girl, don't worry about my dying 'cause God left me with the privilege of caring for and raising you." I need her to take care of me now. I know, when I leave here, I'm going home; not to that house in New Orleans, but to my Grandma's house in Biloxi. At least, I wish I could. I love you, Grandma.

I'm very tired, and I'm ready to go to bed. I don't know where I will be sleeping tonight. I don't know if I'll be sleeping in a chair, on the sofa, or in a bed tonight. As a matter of fact, I don't even know if my own bed still exists or if it's floating somewhere in the Mississippi River. I don't know if my house is under water. I don't know if Tulane is still standing or if I will have a job there for the rest of this semester or ever. Mentally, I understand the situation that I'm in, but the true impact hasn't hit me yet.

I heard someone on the television say that the government defines a disaster as a single small event where the possible lost of life is minimal. What happened to the gulf coast falls under the category of a calamity. I know God creates tragedies in our lives to effect change but I wonder why this tragedy had to equate to a calamity.

Feeling for today: lonely.

Nycki Whiting

Wednesday, August 31, 2005, 7:30 AM

This is a nice neighborhood. This is a nice house, decorated exquisitely and very spacious. Although everyone, even me, is happy to be here, the house isn't big enough to sleep all these people. To keep from being stepped on last night, James and I slept on the dining room floor under the table. I am so glad I grabbed those pillows and blankets before we left New Orleans. At least I learned something from the hurricane parties.

I woke up early to call Raymond, and I finally reached him. At first, he seemed relieved to hear my voice. He said he had been unable to get through on my cell. As soon as I told him that I was at my ex's, he got extremely angry. He screamed at me and accused me of being a two-timing whore. He went on and on and on about how he knew he couldn't trust me, and that was why he hadn't married me. He's been mad at me before, but I don't remember him getting so upset about anything, least of all my being with any of my previous boyfriends. He caught me off guard and I didn't know how to respond.

We were still lying under the table and James heard Raymond ranting. He snatched the phone, pushed the pound button for a long time, and then hung it up. He told me that I better not call Raymond back. Then he jumped up and stormed into the other room. I was so mad at James I could have strangled him. I started to call Raymond back but became mesmerized by story after story of the horrors of the storms aftermath on the big screen television in the adjacent room.

The infrastructure in New Orleans survived Katrina, but it's being washed away now by the flood. In most parts of the city, there is no drinking water, sewer, lights or communication. Desperate people, who under other circumstance were law abiding citizens, are looting and some are stealing televisions. The police are watching and, in some cases, participating. I wonder, is it really a crime to steal food, medicine and other necessities during a calamity?

The Superdome has turned into a hell hole. The numbers have swelled from ten thousand on the day of the storm, to twenty-five thousand people who are barely existing in a stadium without lights or running water. Helicopters are air lifting people from roofs and taking them to the Superdome and to a bridge where they are waiting for further rescue in ninety plus degrees weather. Some rescuers have reported hearing people screaming from their attics. There are hospitals, nursing homes and jails that still need to be evacuated. I didn't hear an estimate of the number of people who are dead but I'm sure it's a lot.

I came into the bathroom to get away from the television reports. (This is the only room without a television blasting.) I'm so confused; I couldn't wait until tonight to write in this journal. In the mist of this calamity, the people that I hated more than anyone in the world have graciously opened their homes and their hearts to me. The person that I love more than anyone in the world has basically abandoned me.

I know that hard times bring out the best in some people, and the worst in others. I also know God has a message for me in all of this. I don't know what He's trying to tell me. However, I do know that, although my world has been turned upside down, I'm blessed to be alive.

Maybe I'll call Raymond back tomorrow.

Feeling for this morning: perplexed but blessed.

Continuation, 10:30 PM

Well, this morning certainly started with a bang. However, the day calmed down after my earlier entry. Today, I've been thinking a lot about God's reason for this calamity.

Last night, James was in a confessing mood. He confessed that, for a long time, he and the ex's have been trying to figure a way to get all of us back together as friends. During undergrad, we were thick as thieves and to tell the truth, I have missed them both. We actually all came to Tulane Law so that we could stay together. I can't believe I've held a grudge for all these years. That's not very Christian, but getting us back together, certainly can't be the reason God created Katrina.

James also confessed that he didn't like Raymond. That certainly wasn't a secret. Although he would never say it, I know James actually hates him. James said that I deserved better and he doesn't understand why I would be involved with someone who treated me so poorly. I wonder the same thing. In fact, that is part of the reason I am seeing Dr. Barbou, but I really didn't want to have that conversation with James, again. I told him I was tired, and wanted to go to sleep. He stretched out his arms and I nestled close to him all night. It felt like an oasis of security in a world of madness. (Instead of calling Raymond this morning, I wish I had stayed in James' arms.)

This afternoon we all went to McDonald's® for lunch. It seems like everyone in our house, and in Baton Rouge, wanted to get away from the news. The restaurants

Unconditional

and streets were packed, and it took us a long time to get back to the house. As soon as we did, every television came on immediately. I was certain that things along the gulf coast were better, but they weren't.

The storm hit on Monday morning. The levees broke Monday night. It is Wednesday and the federal response is still virtually nonexistent. State and local resources are exhausted. It is estimated that of the five hundred thousand people who lived in New Orleans, eighty percent of them evacuated in response to the voluntary order. It seems like the remaining hundred thousand are suffering at the Superdome, on the bridge, wading in the contaminated water, hanging from their roofs, trapped in their attics or dead.

As I watched the television switch between scenes revealing to the world the dire straights of the city, tears began to fall from my eyes. I was not the only person in the house crying. The images on the television were not from a third world country thousands of miles away. They were from a great American city; the city that was now my home. How could this happen? Since 9/11 the President has been espousing how he is beefing up homeland security. WHERE IS IT? WHERE IS THE MILITARY? WHERE IS ANYONE WHO CAN HELP THESE PEOPLE? Why is God letting this happen?

Eventually, I couldn't take anymore. I grabbed my cell phone and went out back to call Raymond. I've called him several times today, but he won't answer. I know what caused him to act the way he did this morning. He was worried. I didn't talk with him on Monday or Tuesday. In fact, other than a few minutes on Sunday, I hadn't talked with him since I left New Orleans. I'll reach him tomorrow and apologize. Everything will be alright. I just wish James wasn't so hard on him.

Feeling for this afternoon: anguish.

PS: Last night, James said he had been waiting for just the right time to discuss the ex-ex's. He was afraid that just mentioning their names would end our friendship. Tomorrow, I'm going to tell him that not even Katrina could do that.

Thursday, September 1, 2005, 10:00 PM

A lot of folks were scheduled to leave this morning; however, most decided to stay one more day. The fellowship is comforting to all of us. In addition, we are beginning to realize that this may be the end of the life that brought us together as friends and the beginning of new lives that none of us planned or requested. We need this time to gather strength for the unknown that we will most certainly have to face.

Although every news outlet is broadcasting, in horrific detail, the dreadfulness of the situation on the gulf coast, the President and his staff appear to be clueless. A few days ago, when the Superdome filled up, officials sent folks to the New Orleans Convention Center. There are approximately ten thousand people waiting there for transport out of the city. No food or water is being provided. Several people have died. Their bodies have been pushed to the side and covered with whatever could be found. The FEMA director said he didn't know they were there until the news start broadcasting the story.

During a news conference this morning, the President told the desperate people in the gulf region to be patient, "help is on the way." He looked down on the region from Air Force One on Wednesday. He will return on Friday to tour the region on the ground. I wonder how many more people will lose their sanity, their hope or their life by then. It probably doesn't matter to him either way.

But it certainly matters to Mayor Nagin. In a radio interview this evening, he used profanity and cried when he sent a public message to the President. He said he didn't want to see anymore press conference. His city was dying.

He needs help and he needs it now. He told Washington to "Get off your asses and let's do something."

The Secretary of Homeland Security said that the response is so slow because no one anticipated the devastation that Katrina caused. However, CNN reported that even before Hurricane Pam was created, scientist warned Washington about New Orleans precarious situation. For years, the Louisiana congressional contingent has requested federal funding to sure up the levees. In the last few years the funds have actually been cut and they, along with the majority of National Guards troops from the region, have gone somewhere else, probably to Iraq.

Meanwhile, by preventing silt from flowing into the ocean from the gulf, the levees existence has contributed to the disappearance of the marsh land and barrier islands on the southern edge of Louisiana. Under God's plan, they would have prevented Katrina from hitting the gulf coast at such a high speed and with such a high sea surge. The Louisiana delegation has also sought funding to rebuild the marsh land and the islands. I wonder if that money is also in Iraq.

To make matters worst, for years man's activities on earth have contributed to global warming. However, no changes have been instituted to effectively decrease the glass house effect. Apparently, the force of Katrina was magnified by the elevated temperature of the ocean. Although I don't fully understand the underlying scientific principles, I know all things in our environment are interrelated. I wonder if the real cause of this calamity is man's alteration of God's planet. Is it possible that God is attempting to reclaim earth and return New Orleans into the river that he intended for it to be? But what about the zillions of other cities that exist because levees and dams channel water bodies in unnatural directions? Why would God ignore them and single out New Orleans? This is probably just some more flawed rationale.

On the other hand, some people have said this is the beginning of the last days. Could this honestly be the beginning of Revelations? Looking at the natural disasters of the last few years -- the five hurricanes that hit Florida last year, the tsunami, Katrina, earthquakes in places not prone to having earthquakes, like Atlanta, AIDS, and the high number of deaths from the bird flu – that theory gives me pause. I'm not sure I believe it but I think, now more than ever, I need to make sure that I am right with God.

My cell phone died and I used someone else's to call Raymond. He answered on the first ring. He must have recognized the New Orleans area code. Surprisingly, he apologized to me for his outburst yesterday. He said he was angry because the military has moved his deployment date up to October. He whined and complained about having to spend Christmas in Germany.

He didn't ask what I was planning on doing since I couldn't go back to New Orleans. I almost asked if I could stay with him in Tallahassee but I decided that I really didn't want to go there after all. I have been asking God if Raymond was what He wanted for me. In hindsight, I think he may have been sending me messages for a long time. Grandma said I was hard headed. Am I so hard headed it took a category five hurricane for me to hear God's answer?

I called my cousin. She was delighted to hear that I would be staying with her and her family in Atlanta for awhile.

Feeling for the day: stupid.

Nycki Whiting

Friday, September 2, 2005, 5:30 PM

Once again, I forgot how to spell cholesterol. We started the day by cooking a big farewell breakfast. Everyone pitched in with the preparations. We fixed salmon crockets, pancakes, scrambled eggs, toast, cheese grits, quiche, sliced fruit, mimosas and a few other froufrou dishes whose names I can't remember. We moved several tables together so that we could all eat in the same room. We designated my ex-ex's as the mother and father of our social unit and demanded that they sit at the ends. James was designated as the spiritual leader and assigned the task of blessing the food. Of course, his prayer referenced Katrina.

Then, in the spirit of Thanksgiving Day, everyone made a statement about this experience and a commitment to one, help a Katrina victim; and two, stay in touch with everyone in the room. (It never dawned on us that we were Katrina victims.) We agreed that we would all leave around one o'clock this afternoon and that until that time no one would turn on the television or the radio or anything that could bring the outside world into our retreat. I think we wanted things to have improved in New Orleans, but we were afraid that they hadn't. Confirmation of that fear would have shattered our hopes for our future.

After we finished eating, everyone reared back in their chairs to let the food settle. James said, as the designated spiritual leader, he needed to know everyone's opinion as to why God made Katrina and allowed her to cause such destruction. We had an hour long discussion in which everyone said basically the same thing a different way and amazingly argued. Eventually, we all agreed that God created Katrina primarily because the world was going to hell in a hand basket. The hurricane was God's way of telling people to be kinder to each other, and it worked. Since Katrina hit, there has been a ground swell of compassion and giving from every sector of the world. James challenged us as individuals to take God's message to heart, and seek out the personal messages that God was sending. He also said that we should let this experience motivate us to divest ourselves of evils that will ultimately be detrimental to our lives and our relationships with God.

Then James said that maybe it would help us to look at things from a different perspective. He asked what if Katrina was an act of the devil, and God being all powerful was using the devil's own actions against the devil. He analogized it to a professional basketball game he had seen several years before. It was when the Bulls were the reigning champs. In the fourth quarter of the last game of one of the Bulls many finals, there was less than one minute on the clock, and the Bulls were down by two points. The ball came in to the guard, and two defenders collapsed on him immediately. The guard dribbled the ball around and around until one of the defenders turned his back to the guard and stood between the guard and the other defender. The guard had literally made the defenders set a screen that gave the guard a clear view of the basket. He made the three point shot and won the game and the championship for the Bulls. James asked what if God is using the devil's act, Katrina, to come in between us and another act of the devil, so that we can have a clear view at the basket, Him. With this clarity we should be able to see where God is directing us. If we follow His direction, we too will win and have a victory.

We sat at the table discussing this theory until about twelve o'clock. Then we cleaned up and tried to put my ex-

ex's house back in its normal state. They both smiled at me when she said it would never be like it was before Katrina, and they never wanted it to be. We all packed, thanked them for their generosity and said goodbye. James was a little tentative walking with me to my car. He asked if we were going to Atlanta. I said certainly as if he had asked a stupid question. I guess I forgot to tell him that I was going to stay with my cousin.

    I called my cousin to tell her that I was on the way. She said that my room was ready and they were waiting for me. She's cooking greens, ham, and sweet potato pie just like Grandma used to make whenever either one of us went home. Although her parents lived down the road from Grandma and me, my cousin stayed with us most of the time. Grandma said that it wasn't right to raise a child without other children in the house. Since me and my cousin were the same age, and she was an only child, Grandma brought her to live with us. We shared a bedroom until we left for college; she slept on the top bunk and I had the bottom.

    When we were little kids and school was out, we played in our dusty front yard from sun up to sun down. We ate breakfast and lunch outside. Grandma would make us come inside for dinner. Lunch was always peanut butter and jelly sandwiches on white bread cut in four on the diagonal. We would pull our sandwiches apart and she would trade her piece of bread with the most jelly for mine with the most peanut butter. It wasn't that she didn't like jelly, but she knew I loved it. She also loved me. She just told me that, in addition to cooking my favorite meal, she's stocked her cabinet with my favorite lunch. She said that we might have to skip the middle man and just make jelly sandwiches without peanut butter. I didn't realize until she said that, how much I miss her.

After I finished talking with her, I called Raymond. He didn't answer. I started to leave a message telling him where I was going and asking him to call me back. But why? My number will be on his missed calls list. If he wants to call me back, he will. He probably won't call. I really don't think I care anymore.

We've been driving for several hours now, and I've spent this time thinking about James' theory, Katrina and my life. I know the clarity that God is providing can be applied to any situation. I'm trying to apply the theory to me.

Feeling for today: new beginnings.

Monday, September 5, 2005, 10:30 PM

It's been several days since I wrote in this journal. Funny, with all that is going on and all that has happened I've been in touch with my feelings. It's actually been an emotional roller coaster. One of the reasons that I haven't written in my journal lately is that after my cousin's family goes to bed, my cousin and I stay up until the wee hours of the morning, talking. Sometimes I cry but I don't think it's solely because I have probably lost all of my belongings. I think I'm crying because it took me so long to come back home. Home is not a certain building or a certain location; it is where your family's located.

When I'm not crying, we're laughing about the things that we did as children and young adults. We laugh a lot and it feels good. I don't think I've laughed this much since we graduated from undergraduate school and moved to different cities. Then there was that thing with the ex's when I got to New Orleans. I let that experience over shadow my relationship with my cousin and my other college friends. The only person that I have kept in contact with is James, and that's because he wouldn't leave me alone. (Thank, God) Nobody stole my joy. I walked away and left it behind.

Speaking of James, he comes over everyday. We spend a lot of time reconstructing our lives. To tell the truth, I don't think I want the life back that I had in New Orleans before Katrina. I'm trying for the life, or at least to become the person I was before Grandma died, but without the guilt. I'm sorry she's gone but I'm glad she lived long enough to see me graduate from Spelman. She kept her promise; she stayed around until I was grown. At least, I was supposed to be grown by that time.

I would love for her to have lived longer, but that wasn't within my control. God decided when it was her time to go. Just like God was ultimately responsible for the death of my parents and brother. I still don't understand why He left me behind, but the reason doesn't matter. What matters is that I had a wonderful, happy childhood with a woman and a cousin who loved me unconditionally.

I now see that James also loves me unconditionally. I've always known I was blessed to have him as a friend. I truly believe that one of the many reasons Katrina struck was to set a screen in front of Raymond so that I could see James clearer. I finally asked him how he learned how to predict the future. After laughing out loud for several minutes, he said that he works hard to keep his mind and soul free from sin so when God talks to him, he can listen. Then he follows God's directions for his life. He isn't a voodoo priest or a psychic. He is just a very well read, observant, spiritual person. He not only believes in God; he is the epitome of "what would Jesus do" and whatever Jesus would do, James does.

My cousin is enamored with him. She asked him why such a wonderful man hadn't found a wife or, at least, a girlfriend. Everyone from our undergrad days, except James and I, are married or have been married at least once. He responded that he is waiting for clarity that he now knows is right around the corner. She laughed and they looked at each other like they were sharing a secret. (I got it but I'm not ready to go there with him . . . yet.)

I almost forgot to write about Raymond. That's because I almost forgot about him period. It hurts when I think about the relationship that I thought we had. I know now that was my fantasy and not his. He called yesterday, but I didn't answer the telephone. He has no idea where I am or who I'm with. I'm tempted to tell him that James and I have finally become lovers. He always thought that was going to happen anyway. I can't lie to get rid of him. I don't know what I'll do about Raymond. Nevertheless, I'm not going to worry about him now.

    I'm too busy getting my life back. Correction, getting a new old life and in my new old life, I'm not sure I want to get married and have children. On second thought, maybe I want to, but I no longer think it's mandatory. Back in the day, whenever that was, women needed a husband to take care of them. In exchange the woman would give up almost everything including her name. I can take care of myself. Plus, I have a family that loves me, and a companion that loves me. I'm not sure I want to trade any of that for a husband. At least, not today but I'll see what tomorrow may bring.

    There are quite a few things that I still need to address. I don't even want to know the condition of my house, but I'm sure it's ruined. However, I'm not going to attempt to recover on my flood insurance policy right now because I'm having a hard time making a list of all of the things I lost. I need my papers to help me remember my liabilities and assets, but I'm sure their ruined also. I work on the list a little everyday and, when things settle down some more, I'm sure I'll be able to complete it. Thank God, I pay bills online. At least, I have an electronic list of most of my creditors.

    Among all of the things that are overwhelming me right now, my cousin's generosity is high on the list. The room she and her husband prepared for me has anything I could possibly want including a few full changes of clothes, a television, a computer and wireless internet service. She put an eight by eleven framed picture of me, her and Grandma standing in front of our house in Biloxi on my dresser. She also made copies of all of her pictures from our childhood and put them in a picture album with a million pictures of her children. (I love those kids. Are they my first cousins once removed or are they my second cousins?). Most likely, my pictures are destroyed. She doesn't know, and I'm not going to tell her, that I haven't looked at my pictures in years.

James and I have a big day planned for tomorrow. We're going to the Red Cross to volunteer. We have to keep the promise that we made in Baton Rouge and, since Tulane is paying us during this break, we feel obligated to help those that are less fortunate. Maybe tomorrow evening I'll feel like writing about Katrina. Discussing America's monumental failure today would destroy the joy that I just resuscitated.

Feeling for the day: cherished.

PS: I watched the Higher Ground Benefit Concert on public television this evening. Danny Glover made the statement that "When the hurricane struck, it did not turn the region into a Third World country - it revealed one." Clarity?

The world breaks everyone . . . and afterwards many are stronger at the broken places.

Ernest Hemingway

Troubled

※

A True Story

I won't let you go; in prayers I'll hold you dear
And when I'm afraid, love will dispel the fear
See I have faith in God that this fight is not in vain
It is my belief in Him that keeps me sane

You are my charge from heaven above
And God equipped me with the weapon of love
Do you think it was by chance that you were placed with me?
Oh no my son, this is where you are meant to be
In a home filled with visions of your success
Surrounded by people willing to give you the very best

With all of my might I will hold on
This race of life you will not run alone
So run on, run on and be what you're called to be
Run on, run on straight into victory

See you are already destined to win
So it doesn't matter how you start —

Because better is the end

© 2005 Shonda Rowe

My heart stopped as I reached into my purse to retrieve the ringing cell telephone. I glanced at the number and in that split second, fear engulfed me. Having been Cameron's mother for the last eleven years, this reaction was common.

"This is Dru," I said.

"Ms. Anderson this is Mr. Brown from the YMCA. I am calling to let you know we are releasing Cameron from the program. The maintenance staff saw him and Logan propping a side door open to sneak out and I saw them getting on a bus. This is not the first time he went missing for a while without explanation. However, this is the first time we have proof. Do you want me to call you when he returns?"

At that moment, I don't know if I was angry, sad, mad or just disappointed.

"No, he doesn't need to call me," I responded.

I proceeded with my doctor's appointment as if I had not just been informed that my son had been released from the Out-of-School Suspension Program: the program for high school students who had been expelled from every other educational setting in the City and County. I filled out the required forms, paid my co-pay, undressed, breathed out and in, dressed, laughed and joked with the doctor and the doctor's staff and scheduled my next mammogram for one year later. When I returned to my car, I called Marion, my husband, then Mackenzie, my daughter, and had the similar conversation with each of them.

"Cameron has been expelled again. I don't know why nor do I care.... What? He will probably runaway. If he does, I won't look for him this time. He will have to come home by himself and at midnight tomorrow, I am discontinuing the service on his cell phone."

After the conversation with my daughter, I called Cameron's cell phone. He didn't answer. I didn't call it again.

Except for a call from Marion later that day informing me that Cameron wasn't at the YMCA for the three o'clock pick up, the rest of my day was routine. I hoped that he would be at home when I returned from work, but I knew he wouldn't. I correctly guessed that after the expulsion earlier that day, he had given up trying to fit into the only family that ever claimed him.

THE BEGINNING

Cameron came to our family one month before the fourth anniversary of the day that the caseworker designated as his birthday and one year before we officially adopted him. His life before that was dreadful. When he was ten months old, in an attempt to thwart an inevitable arrest for shoplifting, his biological mother told the police that she and Cameron were HIV positive. When arrested she also gave conflicting information about Cameron's name, birth date and birth place. After being incarcerated for several weeks, she walked away without retrieving Cameron from the shelter for homeless HIV positive children where he had been placed, or severing her parental rights.

The inaccuracy in the information she provided delayed any hope of Cameron being placed quickly. The state could neither locate his birth certificate nor any family members. The staff of the HIV shelter thinking Cameron had a short life span, made no attempt to prepare him for the challenges of life. Instead he was inundated with everything but love. Ten months later, a follow-up test revealed that Cameron had not contracted AIDS and in fact was not even HIV positive. He was then placed in a series of foster homes. In his last, where he stayed for two years, nurturing was nonexistent and abuse highly suspected. Consequently, during his formative years, Cameron had no opportunity to learn how to love, bond with or trust adults.

Marion and I had made a conscious decision to adopt an older male child from the government agency. Even the state had given up on these children and labeled them "hard to place." We had been blessed with a wonderful daughter, good careers and a beautiful home. Having both been raised in low income homes we felt an obligation to share our success. Our goal was to give a child that would not otherwise have a chance an opportunity at life. We attended all ten of the pre-adoption classes offered by the state which purportedly prepared parents to deal with their adopted children. However, none of them prepared us for the impact that Cameron's placement would make in our lives.

During the first year, Tommy as he was called at the time was so handsome, and despite his behavior, we saw a side of him that was sweet and gentle. He also had a caring nature. We, like so many adoptive families, believed that with enough love Cameron would eventually become the child that we envisioned. Apparently, Cameron didn't understand our vision. In fact, Cameron didn't understand much about himself and neither did we.

From day one, we were in constant battles with him for control. He was consistently defiant and his anger was evident. We initially tried counseling with the female counselor that had been referred by the state adoption agency but after a while it became evident that Cameron was manipulating her with his good looks and charming ways. After that we tried an array of counselors, educational settings, mentoring programs and any activities that we thought would help Cameron live up to our visions. Some of them worked better than others but Cameron managed to get expelled from the majority of them including a very expensive military school that required payment upfront and did not give refunds upon expulsion.

Initially it seemed that much of his unacceptable conduct stemmed from his anger. He was constantly in trouble for his aggressive behavior, including fighting and using profanity which brought negative attention from both his peers and adults. Despite his conduct and any possible fulfillment he received from the attention, I sensed that Cameron was frustrated with always being in trouble. I naively advised him that if he just did the right thing, he would stay out of trouble. It never dawned on me that he didn't know what or how to do the right thing or even that he had never been taught socially acceptable behavior or reactions. Neither Marion nor I considered that, since his formative years were not spent in a loving family or participating in middle class activities like story hour, Mommy and me swimming classes, visits to the zoo or other things to which Mackenzie had been exposed, his thoughts and perceptions were different than ours. In our mind, he was a part of our family. Therefore, he had to adhere to the norms and culture of our household.

With time and counseling he appeared to learn how to control his anger. However, during his teen years, the aggressive behavior resumed. Instead of being rooted in anger, he struggled to maintain his reputation as a formidable combatant. He entered new situations acting as if he were a ghetto thug. He wanted all of his peers to think that he was the coolest and toughness among them. He misrepresented his family size, socioeconomic status and relationship with us and his sister.

He was always big for his age reaching six feet tall by the time he was twelve. However, even with the tough façade, his gentle nature was apparent. The combination of his size and temperament drew the bullies in his direction and if they came, he was certainly not going to back down. That explained some of his fights but some of them were the result of his own bullying. The probable consequences were not enough to deter his aggression. He usually won the fight but was expelled from the program he was involved in at the time.

As he matured his defiance at home subsided. However, he was still apparently defiant and oppositional in other settings. During his teen years, this persistent defiance caused him tremendous problems particularly since he was also easily influenced by the negative pressure of his defiant peers. He didn't distinguish between those kids going in the right direction and those that were engaged in criminal or quasi-criminal activities. He was normally embraced by the later although he had several "good" friends that attempted to keep him out of trouble. However, after a short period of friendship, most of his good friends abandoned him. Time after time, we asked him why he let himself be lead into trouble by bad influences. His response was always, "I don't know."

In the seventh grade, after the expulsion from the military school for fighting, we decided that it was time for Cameron to suffer the consequences of his action. Maybe the shelter of private schools and our efforts to protect him from himself and the "real world" were partially to blame for his defiance. Maybe the neighborhood public school would help him to learn how to behave. He would be forced to deal with all types of children, adults and consequences. Whatever happened, happened and he would have to deal with it. Plus, Mackenzie's transition from a ritzy private school to public school had helped her to become a well-rounded person. Maybe it would have a similar effect on Cameron. After being home schooled for the balance of the year, he was enrolled in the local middle school for the eighth grade.

During his eighth grade year, Cameron's conduct was horrible. He argued with teachers, fought with a number of kids, made the basketball team but never played because of his attitude, smoked marijuana, failed a number of test and classes, bought a gun and bullets to school and fought - no beat up a teacher. At one point during the year, the guidance counselor questioned whether he was depressed and if he suffered from ADHD. He had been diagnosed with both. The counselor convinced us that our resisting giving medication to Cameron was even more detrimental to Cameron than the possible side effects. We inquired with the more effective male psychologist that Cameron was then seeing who prescribed an antidepressant and ADHD medication. His mood improved but his conduct stayed virtually the same.

The school principal, being a middle class parent with a wayward son of his own, felt a kinship to us. He did every thing possible to keep Cameron's school records clean and keep him out of the juvenile justice system where the goal appeared to be destruction instead of rehabilitation. Thus, Cameron was promoted with only a few minor infractions in his school record. He was subsequently admitted to the local high school without question.

THE NINTH GRADE

While this appeared to be fortunate, it wasn't. First, Cameron still was not made to deal with the consequences of his actions. Secondly, we were not made to deal with the unsuitability of the public school environment for an easily influenced and defiant Cameron.

Prior to the commencement of the school year, we considered placing him in a Seven Day Adventist school. The first half of the summer he had attended a tutorial program where the instructor's raved about his excellent academic progress and conduct. However, later that summer, he was expelled after one day at a residential sports camp for his defiance. We questioned his ability to survive in the strict environment of a fundamentalist Christian school. However, we did not make a final decision at that time.

Fearful of leaving him home alone during the day for the rest of summer, we enrolled him in basketball and football training at the neighborhood high school. We were impressed with the coaching staff's ability to control Cameron and Cameron's devotion to football. The coaches were committed to sustaining a team of stellar student athletes. Hoping the lure of playing sports would be enough to keep him out of trouble and focused on his school work, we enrolled him in public school again.

We were unaware that his "cousin," Connor, a boy with whom Cameron had been friends since kindergarten and with whose mother we were friends, was dealing drugs, stealing cars and committing other serious crimes. Another friend had told us Connor's mother had been having problems with him for a while. We did not know how serious the problems were until a week before school started when Connor got drunk while spending the night at our house.

Afterwards we told Cameron to stay away from Connor. However, Cameron admired Connor. Cameron believed that, although Connor was committing crimes, he wouldn't let Cameron get hurt or in trouble. Despite our directions, Cameron spent most of his time at the new school with Connor. The football coach, who had high hopes for Cameron and his natural athletic ability but thought, like the rest of the teachers, staff and many of the students at the school, that Connor was useless, informed us of the association. They also warned Cameron about associating with Connor.

The coach punished Cameron for skipping practice by making him sit out of the following game. Cameron skipped most practices to hang with Connor. During the entire football season, Cameron played in only one game although he was a member of the ninth grade, junior varsity and on the third string of the varsity team. Cameron could not see that his association with Connor, who had been banned from sports in his freshmen year for smoking marijuana on campus, was destroying his opportunity.

Meanwhile, Cameron was failing all of his core courses. Like so many times before, I naively resorted to internet psychology and tried to structure punishments and encouragements to get Cameron on the right track. Because Cameron was also falling asleep in class, I researched the side effects of his medication and enrolled in a sleeping problem workshop which I never attended. I ignored the warnings on the WebPages that instructed concerned parents to rule out drug use as a cause for a teen's sleep problems before seeking out any other solutions. We started giving him his medication at night instead of in the morning. I believed Cameron when he told me he was not smoking marijuana.

One evening, while leaving a football game that he, of course, did not dress for, Cameron was confronted by a boy he didn't know. Cameron did not back down from the threat. The police officer directing traffic saw the commotion and stopped the fight. Cameron, not wanting to be suspended from school for ten days, attempted to avoid a subsequent fight with the boy by reporting the incident to his coaches and another police officer. However, when the police officer asked him to identify the boy, he refused to do so saying that his cousin would take care of it.

For an entire week Cameron went to classes only if accompanied by his "boys." Of course, his main "boy" was Connor. We coincidentally found out about the continuing conflict while attending an unrelated meeting at the school. We spoke with the police officer who promised to bring the boys together and work things out. A few days later, I asked Cameron about the matter. He told me that it was all worked out.

However, the next day while in the lunch room, Cameron argued with the boy. When he attempted to walk away, the boy jumped him from behind. Cameron was getting the best of the fight until the boy's friends pulled Cameron's feet from under him. Cameron's head hit the concrete floor. When I saw the school's number on my cell phone, before I even answered, I knew Cameron was in trouble again.

An ambulance brought Cameron to the hospital where Mackenzie and I were waiting. The doctor examined him and determined he had a fractured skull. He was placed in intensive care. Although he was extremely angry, he would not disclose to me or Evan, Mackenzie's fiancé, why the boy wanted to fight him or if his relationship with Connor had anything to do with the fight.

Cameron was released from the hospital a week later. The doctor, appalled at the inability of the school to prevent such occurrences, ordered Cameron not return to that school. Another head injury could result in permanent injury or death and I knew Cameron would not be able to resist fighting the boy, his friends or anyone who teased him about getting hurt. Thinking that his conduct had improved, we applied to the Seven Day Adventist School that we had considered at the beginning of the summer. At least the peer influence there would be better than at the public school.

Mackenzie, who had a Degree in Chemistry, was a stay at home Mom at the time. She had been a substitute teacher the previous school year. For the next three months, she home schooled Cameron in the new school's curriculum. Cameron's didn't like the work and his efforts were minimal. He clandestinely stayed in contact with Connor. When Connor suggested that he runaway to get out of doing the school work, Cameron did.

Marion, Mackenzie and I looked everywhere for him. We called him and text messaged him at least a hundred times. He didn't answer our calls until Mackenzie called from a number he didn't recognize. After much negotiation, he allowed her to pick him up from the local transit station. Even though he was staying with Connor at night, Connor's mother never contacted me. However, Cameron spent his days with friends that I approved.

In January of the following year, we enrolled him in the Seven Day Adventist School. He appeared to be doing well. Although he had a slow start, his grades were rising and he seemed to be making "good" friends. We begin to exhale until the end of February, when he came home with a story about a boy smoking cigars in the bathroom and attempting to place the blame on Cameron. The next day Marion received the call. The boy confronted Cameron, they fought and Cameron was expelled from yet another school.

We were livid. We pointed out to him that although he won the fight, he was the loser. The likelihood that he would finish the ninth grade before the beginning of the next school year was slim. He seemed to finally understand how this fight as well as all of his previous fights had hurt him. This incremental improvement, gave us hope. So we gave him yet another chance.

We allowed him to be home schooled again with the admonishment that in the fall he would be a sophomore at an Adventist School. That meant he would have to spend all of his time doing school work. To provide a diversion, we instituted weekly family dinner and family outings. We also allowed him to continue in the church choir, bible study, Sunday school and A-team, a support group for adoptive teens that met monthly. Other than that, he would have no activities, not even talking on the phone.

That following Thursday while Cameron was at bible study, a neighbor told me that Cameron and a fair skinned boy with curly hair were smoking marijuana in front of the house. Even without the description, I knew it was Connor. A few months earlier, Connor's mother had demanded that he participate in family counseling. He refused, walked out of the house, and moved in with his ninety year old, blind, widowed grandmother where there was no structure or supervision. He had not been to school since he left his mother's house.

I was livid, again. I pulled Cameron from bible study, brought him home and commenced beating him with a broom that was handy. By this time, Cameron was over six feet tall and two hundred, ten pounds. Although, overweight, I knew there was no way I could inflict effective corporal punishment on him by hand. However, before I got in the second lick, Cameron walked out of the house and returned to church. When bible study was over, the youth pastor asked Cameron why no one was there to pick him up. Cameron said he wasn't going home. The youth pastor wouldn't let him leave. He could not find our home telephone number and Cameron refused to give it to him. He did find Mackenzie's number and called her.

Having been advised of his smoking, at first she refused to pick him up. Eventually, her anger subsided. She brought him to her house and then called me. When I arrived, I gave Cameron a choice, go on and leave or take a beating with a broom. Cameron chose the broom. I spanked him. I told him, just like I had told him a million times before; he had to let me parent him.

The next day, I enrolled Cameron in the Out-of-School Suspension Program at the YMCA. After the marijuana incident we warned him, in the presence of the psychologist, that he had no more chances. There was no way he could continue to live in our house unless he could follow the rules and stay in school. The warning obviously worked, for a while. The staff at the YMCA repeatedly told me about his good character. They wanted him to work in the summer camp and to attend a private mentoring program ran by one of the counselors. The Pastor also commented on his improvement. Even when I failed to update his home school assignments, Cameron moved ahead and managed to earn a "B" average in two of his four subjects. His schedule was tight and the workload was heavy but Cameron seemed to be handling it. We cautiously breathed a sigh of relief.

A CHANGE IN ATTITUDE

Then something happened. I played the scenario over and over in my head trying to pinpoint when things begin to change. What had happened to turn him back in the wrong direction? Was it the move out of the townhouse that we lived in temporarily back into the house that we had moved from six months earlier? Was it Mackenzie's breakup with her fiancé which was the impetus for the move? Was it because Mackenzie and her ten month old son would be living in the big house with the rest of the family? Was it the volatile adjustment period during the reunification of the family? Was it the reduction in attention that I paid Cameron during the move? Or was it something that had nothing to do with the family? Was he again the victim of poor peer pressure and being easily influenced? Or, even though the improvement was more significant this time than ever before, was this the same old same old: get in trouble; stay on the straight and narrow for a few months, then get in trouble again?

I pondered these questions for a full three days while Cameron remained absent from home. After his release from the Out-of-School Suspension Program, Cameron made no attempt to contact us and we made no attempt to contact him. However, we kept tabs on his whereabouts. The day after he left, I reported his absence to the police and called the YMCA to see if they knew where he was. They reported that he was with Logan, the boy that he had skipped out of the YMCA with the day before. I wondered what mother would let a child stay overnight in her home without talking with his parents. I later found out that Cameron had one of his older friends call Logan's mother and pretend she was his mother. They concocted a story that his parents were going out of town and wanted Cameron to stay with Logan so that he would not miss days at the program.

By Friday, fearful of the side effects of his abruptly stopping the antidepressant, we sought the assistance of the police to deliver his medication to him. First, I called the youth division of the local police department attempting to locate the investigator to whom our case was assigned. After leaving several messages, I was finally connected to an investigator. He listened to the first half of my story and then put me on hold for an hour. I decided that maybe a face to face would be more productive.

At the police station, I was confronted by the Sergeant who acted like he couldn't understand what I was talking about. Eventually, he said he couldn't deliver the medicine. He did agree to call the YMCA and get the address of the house where Cameron was staying since the program director would not release the information to me.

The Sergeant called once and was told that the program director was out of town. When he was unable to speak with the right person, he told me to come back on Monday. I again explained to him the urgency of getting the medicine to Cameron. It was obvious that I was interfering with something he was doing. He continued to try to brush me off and I persisted to no avail. Eventually I left. I informed Marion that if we wanted help from the police, we would have to use our connections.

Marion called the police commissioner's cell phone. Within thirty minutes both of us received several calls from the police youth squad. Within an hour two investigators went to the YMCA to get the address. By eight o'clock that evening, the police had picked up Cameron and called to make arrangements to return him to us. Because the police were acting outside of their jurisdiction when they apprehended him, they asked that we meet them at a gas station just outside the city limits. Cameron had come with the police officers without resistance and he peacefully came with us.

On the way home, I asked Cameron if he was coming with us because he wanted to or because the police made him. I knew Cameron had changed when he responded, "Do you want the truth? . . . because the police made me." It had been a long week and Marion and I were exhausted. In addition we needed time to digest all that had happened that day. We decided to discuss the matter over breakfast.

When Cameron entered the room the following morning, he was defiant and disrespectful. I asked him what he thought should happen. He wanted to go back to the YMCA, forget the home school and start the ninth grade over in September at the neighborhood public school. He said the home schooling was too much work and he was never going to work that hard again. He also felt that if he was able to get back into the program at the YMCA, he should not have any repercussion for running away. I asked him why he had left the YMCA although I had all but forgotten that was the impetus behind his running away. His response was simply, "I didn't feel like being bothered with the teacher because I was tired. So I just left."

Several times before, we threatened to send Cameron to an Outdoor Treatment Program. When the topic came up this time, for a split second, Cameron seemed distressed. However, his expression quickly returned to deadpan like it always was when he was being scolded. He didn't seem to realize this time the circumstances were different. He had gotten released from his fifth program in the last year. With his previous infractions there were always some redeeming factors to convince us that Cameron had just made a stupid mistake from which he learned a valuable lesson. This time there were no such factors. Conversely, his attitude, mannerisms and comments indicated that the incremental improvements of the last three years were reversed. He was now using his energy to do the wrong thing and in the process assure that he would be absolutely and permanently severed from our home and family. I refused to believe that that was what he really wanted.

After our discussion, Cameron went to his room to finish unpacking from the family's move. He was reserved but appeared to be complying with our request. Later that day, Marion took Cameron with him to run errands. When they returned, Cameron's attitude was remorseful. When I inquired, at first he responded that he was OK. I pressed further. He blurted out that he hated his father because he said that he would not be able to go to the YMCA. He said he didn't care about anything or anybody if he couldn't go back to the YMCA.

In fact, he didn't want to be a part of our family or

live in our house anymore. He said that he wasn't like us and every time he came home he thought about all of the bad things he had done in the last three years, none of which he was sorry about. He went on to say that when he was at Logan's house, he didn't feel bad. Logan's mother, Ms. Smith accepted him for whom he was and she knew how to make her children responsible. We made things too easy for him. Plus she never fussed. Everyone in our house fussed too much and there was always confusion.

He was unaware of a telephone call that I received earlier that week from one of the staff members at the YMCA. She advised me that Logan and his brother were trouble and had been in serious trouble a number of times before. Ms. Smith was a single mother of five teenagers. She worked two full time jobs and had little or no time for child rearing. I surmised that no matter what he said, Cameron felt better in an environment where there were not expectations and no rules. I often wonder if the following events would have been different if I had pointed out that he had given up on himself.

Cameron decided to leave. He asked Marion if he could take the clothes that he purchased. Marion, who was doing the yard work, traditionally Cameron's responsibility, screamed "hell no." He told Cameron that if he were going to leave, he needed to leave with the clothes on his back. I tried to convince Cameron that we loved him and that his life would be much easier if he stayed with us until he graduated from high school; there was nothing that would make him stay. Cameron kissed me and his nephew goodbye and walked out of the door. Mackenzie, who had said to let him go, was surprised that he left. I wasn't. I explained to her that Cameron and I never had the type of relationship that she and I had. For the first time since this family crisis begun, she expressed her anger with him and his treatment of us.

About an hour later, Cameron called to say he had arrived at Ms. Smith's as if we had given him permission to spend the night with a friend. Later that evening when the boys were not around, Ms. Smith called me back. I told her what had transpired at our house that afternoon and asked if Cameron could stay with her for a few days. I needed time to secure placement for him in a program. After I promised to compensate her, she agreed.

I spent the following day, which coincidentally was mother's day, wondering about the safety and sanity of my son. When he left the night before he had promised to come and visit me for mother's day. When he did not come, I cried off and on all day. I also wondered if this was the time to let him go. I had heard so many stories about adopted children who, at the brink of adulthood, walked away from their adopted families and never returned. Mentally I grasped the concept; emotionally it was incomprehensible.

Cameron, Logan, and Logan's brother spent the entire day roaming the streets. They started in the morning heading to our house for mother's day but several circumstances prevented their arrival. First, a homeless man agitated them at the train station. They tried to ignore him but eventually he became unbearable. The three of them beat him up. The transit authority police office was familiar with the man and knew that he habitually instigated fights with the riders. The police officer released the boys with an admonishment for them to go home. They didn't.

Instead, they roamed the streets until after one o'clock in the morning never making it to our house or any of the other locations that they had planned to visit. They attempted to catch the last bus back to Logan's house. They didn't realize that the weekend schedule was different. The last bus had left thirty minutes before they arrived. When they called Ms. Smith to pick them up, she was not only tired but annoyed by their unexplained absence. She told them that if they were men enough to stay away all day without permission, they must also be men enough to find their own way home. Consequently, they went into a car rental office planning to steal a car. Because they, at least Cameron, were virtual instead of actual thugs, they were caught immediately, arrested and taken to the state's child services agency.

As soon as permitted, Logan and his brother called their mother, told her where they were and begged her to come get them. Cameron did not call home. Instead he told the caseworker that Ms. Smith was his aunt and that he had been staying with her for two weeks. When the case worker asked Ms. Smith about Cameron, she said he wasn't hers and she did not want him. Cameron still did not give the caseworker any information about us.

The following morning, on my way to the office, I called Ms. Smith to check on Cameron. She started the conversation by saying, "Let me give you a telephone number." Afterwards she relayed the part of the story that she knew and advised me to call the caseworker for the rest. I called immediately but before the caseworker would discuss Cameron with me, I had to convince her that I was his mother. I was stunned when she asked, in an incredulous tone, if I wanted him back.

The following day, Marion and I attended a conference at which the state was to determine whether or not they would recommend to the Juvenile Court that custody of our son be returned to us. We arrived at the hearing at the scheduled time of noon and were directed to a waiting room where we sat for thirty minutes. We later learned that the start of the conference was delayed because Cameron, Logan and his brother, who were being brought to the conference from a group home, jumped out of the state's van and ran. They had also run from the group home the night before but were returned when a very observant nurse noticed that they were trying to sleep in a hospital lobby.

The conference began with his caseworker reading the charges that the police had filed against him. The story of his antics during the previous day, as well as his actions from the previous week, all seemed surreal to me. Was Cameron doing these things? The vision that Marion and I had of him eleven years ago had long since been replaced by a simple desire that Cameron finish high school. It was beginning to look like he would not even accomplish that.

I was asked to describe the circumstances that led to his being taken into the state's custody. I described our past efforts with Cameron and disclosed our future plans. When requested I read, from his latest psychological evaluation, the diagnosis of "Adjustment Disorder with a Disordering of Conduct." The axis list included defiance disorder, ADHD and chronic depression. I had read this evaluation a million times in the past. During this current crisis the diagnosis took on a different meaning. I re-researched the disorders on the internet. This time I could not align the symptoms of Adjustment Disorder with Cameron's behavior now or in the past.

At the end of the meeting, the lead caseworker commended us on our efforts with Cameron and on the fact that we had not given up on him. After the meeting, we went to our respective offices. Naturally we were concerned about Cameron and could not image what would have made him run away from child services. Within the hour, my cell phone rang. This time I didn't cringe in fear. Instead, I quickly looked at the number and answered the phone immediately.

It was the pastor telling me that Cameron and Logan were at our church asking for money to catch the bus back to Logan's house. No one knew where Logan's brother had gone. I asked the pastor to detain him until I arrived. When I arrived at the church both boys were sitting in the pastor's office. They looked grubby and unkempt. Cameron was not happy to see me. He decided to come home only after I agreed to let Logan spend the night. His attitude was still defiant and disrespectful.

The custody hearing for both boys was scheduled at nine o'clock in the morning the following morning. Cameron knew about the hearing and he also knew that it was not a good idea to miss a court date. As soon as we got home, he began to prepare himself and Logan for the hearing. He suggested that they get hair cuts and that they wear something other than the baggy clothes that was their uniform. He laid out his church suit and his church shoes and instructed Logan to call his mother to tell her to bring him some dress clothes. He acted as if he had years of experience in the judicial system when in fact this was only his second time ever being in a court room. He also didn't seem to realize or care that this was the hearing at which he would be returned to our custody.

ATTACHMENT VS ADJUSTMENT

I was impressed with the level of maturity he displayed in his preparation for court. Under any other circumstance, I would have complimented him. However, even that small development was cancelled out when he announced, as if it was common place, that during his child services examination, the doctor suspected that he had contracted a sexually transmitted disease. I skipped past asking him had he been having sex and dove straight into a lecture about AIDS and unprotected sex. I had to muster up great amounts of self-control to keep from screaming or slapping Cameron across the face.

On the way to the hearing, I received an email on my blackberry from one of the treatment programs that I had applied to for Cameron. The email asked if Cameron had "attachment disorder?" I responded "yes," then proceeded to Juvenile Court to reclaim custody of my son.

When we arrived, the caseworker again commended us for not giving up on Cameron. She withdrew the custody matter and learned that the police had not filed the car theft charges. The result was that Cameron was free to go. Cameron was quiet as we left the court. He appeared to be upset because he thought hat Logan was going to be sent to the detention center. Ms. Smith had indicated that he was on probation for an earlier infraction. However, Cameron went to the YMCA and remained there until Marion picked him up at three o'clock that afternoon.

While going to my office from Juvenile Court, I wondered why the treatment program had asked me about attachment disorder. Cameron's diagnosis was on the front page of the latest evaluation. I had sent it along with his

Unconditional

other three reports to the program. The admission officer had indicated that the evaluation team had reviewed all four evaluations. How could they have missed the diagnosis?

Concerned that there had been some mistakes, I pulled out the report which I had been carrying in my briefcase for the last week. I realized that the report said "adjustment" and not "attachment." I reviewed the symptoms of both disorders on the internet. I discovered the circumstance of Cameron's early life were the primary cause of attachment disorder. Cameron also exhibited ninety percent of the other symptoms. I emailed Marion and within minutes he responded that the attachment disorder diagnosis was on point. While at one time it may have been accurate, adjustment disorder seemed an improper diagnosis. I emailed the program and explained my earlier mistake, indicated that attachment disorder seemed a more appropriate diagnosis than adjustment disorder, and promised to discuss the latter diagnosis with Cameron's counselor.

By reading further, I learned that reactive attachment disorder, or RAD as it is sometimes called, did not respond to traditional therapy. That discovery made me cry. I was not sure if it was from anger with the psychologist or sorrow for Cameron. Cameron had been in traditional therapy off and on for the entire time he had been with us. For the last three years, he had been in consistent therapy with a psychologist the family trusted. While there had been improvement, the bad/good/bad pattern remained constant. I emailed the counselor asking if Cameron had RAD. He never responded.

Some of the characteristics of RAD are an inability to trust adults, a keen ability to manipulate and a strong need to control everything around them. Looking back with that knowledge, I was better able to understand Cameron's conduct. My resolve increased and I knew that placing Cameron in a program with a component dedicated to RAD was mandatory. I contacted two educational consultants who gratuitously gave me advice on several facilities which I promptly checked out. I settled on one in Utah since it is one of few states in the country that can legally force a child to remain in a program until age eighteen.

Meanwhile, Cameron's conduct and attitude were sporadic. He would fluctuate from the mild mannered, compliant Cameron that he had been prior to the expulsion at the YMCA, to the belligerent defiant person who had been brought back to us by the police the week before. Knowing our plans for him, we agreed to tolerate his attitude until we were able to get him securely placed in a program. We felt that was the only way to keep him from running to a place where we might not be able to find him.

However, when he refused to participate in family dinner choosing instead to wash my car, I just about reached my limits. However, the real breaking point came when Cameron, instead of just backing the car out of the garage into the driveway, choose to drive the car around the cul-de-sac, stopping and blasting the music in the center of the circle. Fearing that Cameron was preparing to steal the car, Marion ran out and ordered him back in the driveway.

Fearing that Marion was going to kill or seriously harm Cameron, I went out in the driveway and announced that they both should come to the family meeting right then. After a few minutes, Marion and I regained our composure. We remembered that it was important to keep Cameron in place until the placement could be secured. I asked Cameron to assist us in establishing rules to which he felt he could adhere.

Cameron half heartedly participated in the exercise. The information that he did reveal exposed the irrationality of his thought pattern. First, he felt he should have more independence. He had no response for our questions regarding suitable punishment for running away from home and from child services. He couldn't understand that independence was a privilege that he would earn only if we trusted him. His recent antics had obviously destroyed our trust.

Second, he proclaimed that he would never work as hard as he did with the home schooling. That was way too much work for him. He did not acknowledge that the home schooling was really a concession that had been made because of his inability to remain in school.

Third, he announced that if we put him in private school he would be miserable and get kicked out. To this, we reiterated an earlier agreement, that if he went to a treatment program, participated fully and graduated we would consider his going to public school. He didn't like that arrangement but when asked, he did not have an alternative other than going to a public school outside of our district.

Finally, he wanted to work to earn his own money but since we were saving money for him, he didn't need to save. Cameron didn't flinch when I informed him that all of the money in his savings had been removed and would never be returned. He also didn't flinch when I told him that I would never pay for him to have another cell phone.

At the end of the meeting, trying to appear as if the crisis was over, I ordered Cameron to resume his home school work in those courses that he had obtained a "B." At first, Cameron said "what for?" And then he tacitly agreed. He went upstairs in his room where he stayed until the next morning when I asked him to assist me with chores. While doing the chores, I started to lecture him about whom and what he wanted to become. However, it was clear that he wasn't absorbing anything I was saying.

It was also evident that he was buying time until he could leave again which he did later that day while I was running errands and his sister was during a promotion at the local mall. He packed his "cool" clothes in bags, placed them in his sister's car and drove to Connor's grandmother's house. On his way out of the house he picked up a large, half full bottle, into which his sister had thrown coins since she learned of her pregnancy twenty months earlier. While I was out, he called me twice. I suspect he called first when he took the car and then when he returned it.

When I returned home, I knew immediately that he was gone. In fact, I suspected that he would be gone even before I left. I had started to demand that he come with me but decided if he was going to go, I wanted him to leave on a day when I was not at work. I was honestly afraid of what he might do or take if he knew he had a set amount of time before one of us returned. As it was, other than his clothes and his sister's bank, he only took his discontinued cell phone and a set of keys. Due to the uncertainty of his temperament, the following morning we had all of the locks to the house re-keyed.

It wasn't difficult to determine how he had left or where he had gone. He failed to return the baby's car seat to its normal place in the car. He also left the keys to the other family cars in the floor of his sister's car. Apparently, he didn't' know which key was the proper one for her car and had taken all of them out of the house. Determining that he was at Connor's was a matter of reasonable deduction. There was simply nowhere else for him to go.

THE DECISION

After Cameron left our house three times in three weeks, Marion and I begin to question our decision to place Cameron in a treatment program. Maybe it was time to just let him go. The treatment programs were extremely expensive. We had considered either withdrawing funds from our retirement account or borrowing the funds. Either way, my dreams of retiring early would vanish. On the other hand, forcing him to come home was not an option. Even if he came home on his own, we would have to consider whether or not we felt comfortable with him in our house with his current disposition.

Based on several comments he made during the brief periods he was home, we hypothesized many different scenarios regarding his proclivity to leave home. Had he become a gang member or a pawn for some criminal enterprise? Had the older friend who pretended she was me when he ran away from the YMCA turned him out and he felt he had to be with her? Because he was at Connor's, we wondered if maybe he was too far into the drug use or the criminal underworld for us to recover him.

But in the final analysis, we decided there really wasn't any choice. Cameron was only fifteen and he was our son. On top of that, he had spent most of his life participating in therapy which did not address his core issues. No matter what he had done or what he was involved in, he still deserved a fair chance at life.

We feverishly worked on securing the placement and lining up escorts to take him to Utah. We also worked on keeping a handle on Cameron's location. The latter wasn't very difficult because Cameron continued to attend the YMCA and his activities at our church which was located directly behind our house. In fact, on the Tuesday after Cameron moved in with Connor and his grandmother, Marion and I saw him as we left our weekly Weight Watchers class held at the church.

He was wearing pants so big that he had to pull them up every other step. I didn't realize that it was Cameron until we had driven past him. We stopped him just before he entered the front door of the church. He was going to attend choir rehearsal. I asked him all of the typical mother questions: how he was doing, where he was staying and what was he eating. He responded in his usual mild mannered, compliant tone that he was alright. He said he was staying with "R." Of course, we knew that "R," was his secret name for Connor. I asked him what he was doing for money and he confessed to taking his sister's money jar.

I reminded him that he could come home if he was willing to live by our rules. I asked him if he wanted to come home. He responded "Not yet." Then I told him that we loved him and we said goodbye. Although he indicated he wasn't ready, I sensed that he really wanted to come with us. However, I was still determined to make him own up to walking out on his family. He needed to come home on his own.

As we drove away, we decided to have Cameron put in detention until we could secure placement for him. Earlier that week, I had obtained an order from the Juvenile Court which we thought provided the legal basis for us to have the police arrest him. As a lawyer, I knew that if we refused to accept him when the police brought him to our house, they would charge us with child neglect. However, he would then be taken to detention. I was certain that I could get the charges against Marion and I dismissed by explaining to the Judge that getting him put in detention was the only way we could hold him until the placement.

We left the church and headed directly to the police station where we learned that the order was basically useless. In the state's eyes, if a parent knows their child's location, the child is in the parent's custody. Therefore, because we, his parents, were reporting his location he was no longer a runaway and the police did not have a legal right to apprehend him. When we left the police station, I stuck the order in the sun visor on the passenger's side of my car and forgot about it.

Earlier while we were talking with Cameron in front of church, my cell phone rang. I looked at the number, noticed the Utah area code and declined the call. On the way from the police station, I returned the call. I had already received a rejection notice from the earlier program because they were not equipped to deal with attachment disorder.

When I reached the admission officer of the Utah program he explained that the program in Utah had two therapists trained in attachment disorder therapy. However, the primary therapy came during peer group sessions. The program participants also received one hour per week of counseling with a professional therapist. During a stay that lasted nine to twelve months, the program participants moved through three levels to obtain graduation. At each level the participant was permitted to earn more privileges and given a greater level of responsibility. The admission officer advised me that they currently had four openings and if I was interested, I should download the application from their webpage and fax it back as soon as possible. Within one hour after arriving home, I completed and submitted the required documents.

The next evening, I was astonished when I answered the telephone and Cameron asked me if he could spend the night at Logan's. Ms. Smith and I had remained in contact. She refused to let him stay unless he obtained permission from me. My response proved true the old adage "What a difference a day makes?" No matter how unsupervised that environment, it was better than his staying with drug dealing Connor. I suggested and he agreed to stay there until he was ready to come home. He also agreed to come home on Saturday night so the family could go to church together on Sunday morning.

Unbeknownst to all of us, Ms. Smith had made arrangements to place Logan and his brother in the state's boot camp. On the following day, she took Cameron with her to Juvenile Court where she relinquished custody of her boys to the state. Cameron stood silently as the youth officers took the boys away. On the way home, Ms Smith stopped by the store and asked Cameron to go in for her. While he was in the store, she called, told me what happened and told me she was dropping Cameron at church for youth bible study. She also indicated that she had grown weary with Cameron. Not wanting to lose her as a source in our quest, I told her that I would get Cameron from bible study and bring him home.

I called Marion who was on a business trip on the other side of the country, updated him and expressed how much I was dreading picking up Cameron. It wasn't that I didn't want him home, but it was Thursday. The escorts were tentatively scheduled to come on Saturday. I didn't want to spend the next few days trying to pretend things were normal while at the same time trying to keep tabs on him. I didn't even know if I could pretend that things were normal. The truth was after three weeks of his coming and going. I really didn't know what normal was particularly since I would be afraid that he would walk out any minute. We decided that the best course of action was for me to keep him in my presence until the escorts or Marion arrived on Saturday. I prayed Cameron would cooperate.

As I entered the church the youth pastor, was standing at the door. We spoke for a brief moment and he directed me to a hallway where Cameron was supposed to be calling his ride. His wasn't there. After searching the church for a few minutes we discovered a back door out of which he must have slipped. The pastor said that Cameron came to bible study, did not participate, laid his head on the table and fell asleep. When the pastor woke him he was belligerent and abusive. When the pastor escorted him out of the room, he told the pastor he didn't care about getting kicked out. In fact he didn't care about anything.

The pastor was certain that Cameron was under the influence of some drugs. I couldn't understand how and where Cameron could have gone to smoke marijuana between the time Ms. Smith dropped him at church and the beginning of Bible Study. It never dawned on me that he could have taken a less obvious intoxicant like methamphetamine. I was convinced that more than likely, the experience of seeing his friends being taken away to boot camp had intensified his already desperate frame of mind.

I knew he was headed to Connor's grandmother's house but I did not attempt to apprehend him. Instead I went home and called Marion. Mackenzie listened while I told Marion about the incident. When I hung up the telephone she said that Marion and I didn't deserve the things that Cameron had done to us. Then she stormed out of the kitchen. From that point on she refused to be involved with any of our efforts to apprehend Cameron and get him placed. Although I understood her feelings, I hoped that she would not give up on Cameron, particularly since he had indicated a number of times how much he loved her and how glad he was that she was his sister.

THE APPREHENSION

With the escorts scheduled to arrive in two days and the time period for placement limited to two weeks, it was imperative that we locate and apprehend Cameron. For this purpose, it was fortunate that Cameron had over used his cell phone prior to it being discontinued. The thirty-six page bill that I received in the mail earlier that week listed everyone he had called for the thirty day period before he ran away. As I reviewed it for numbers that appeared over and over again, I concluded that the running away was a culminating event and not the commencement of the change.

Coincidentally, earlier that week, an investigator from the Juvenile Court had called me requesting that Cameron be a witness in the case of one of the boys that jumped him at school. The subpoena arrived in the mail that morning. I used that information as an entree into discussions with his friends and their parents. I started by calling the numbers that appeared several times on the cell phone bill. Eventually, I reached a young woman who was the sister of a girl named Mackenzie. Cameron had told me he liked a girl who had the same name as his sister. He had also showed me a picture of her on a teen internet webpage.

I told Mackenzie's sister that, four weeks before that night, Cameron had runaway and I needed him to know about the subpoena. After disclosing that she had given him and a very disrespectful, curly hair boy a ride she gave me her mother's cell phone number. She also advised me to get Cameron away from that other boy because he was bad news. I laughed to myself.

I called Mackenzie's mother and told her simply that we were trying to apprehend Cameron to send him to a program. I didn't go into detail about the location, length or kind of the program. When I disclosed this information to his other girlfriend, Lila's mother, she recoiled. I was uncertain about her loyalty to our efforts. I knew not to make that mistake again. Luckily, Mackenzie's mother wanted to get Mackenzie away from Cameron as badly as we wanted to apprehend him. She ordered Mackenzie to cooperate. However, I have no doubt that Mackenzie would have participated even if not ordered. While Cameron's seemed to make extremely poor choices in male friends, all of his girlfriends appeared to be good girls, most with good grades and all with good parents that adhered to the same or similar middle class values and principles as our family.

That evening, I also engaged the services of a local private detective who knew the city and had connections to both the city and the county police departments. One hour after my discussion with Mackenzie, the girlfriend, she called back and gave me two telephone numbers: one where Cameron called from and the other was a call back number he gave her. I inserted both numbers in a reverse telephone directory that I located on the internet. The results confirmed my suspicion. Cameron was with Connor. The call back number was to a cell phone listed in the name of one of Connor's fellow drug dealers.

I called the private detective to have Cameron

apprehended but couldn't locate the pick up order. I then decided it was best to wait for the escorts to arrive on the next day because I had a confirmed handle on his whereabouts. If he was returned to me, he may have run to a location where I could not find him. I called Marion, updated him and, since we were pretty certain we could find Cameron, he confirmed the escorts coming.

Marion arrived home from his business trip at 5:30 am on Saturday morning. He did not rest on the airplane and did not go to bed when he got home. The private investigator and my cousin, Carl who had offered to assist us, arrived at the house around ten o'clock in the morning. After determining that it would be best to locate Cameron but not pick him up until the escorts arrived at approximately two o'clock that afternoon.

The private investigator put surveillance onto Connor's house and then his daughter called it and asked to speak to Cameron. Connor's grandmother, desperate for company, began a conversation. She disclosed that Cameron had stayed at the house the night before but left about thirty minutes earlier. Connor had gone out of town with friends. During the surveillance of the house, two known drug dealers came to the house. One of them fit the description of Cameron and, although we had not indicated or suspected that Cameron was dealing, the private investigator understood that parents are sometimes blind or in denial regarding their children's activities.

The night before, Cameron indicated to Mackenzie that he might be staying with Connor's drug dealing friend. We knew where he lived but didn't know the address. Therefore, while the investigator was watching Connor's house, Marion and Carl attempted to locate the house. They were going to survey it to see if Cameron was there.

Meanwhile, I remained home which we were jokingly calling central control. First, I checked with Ms. Smith who told me that Cameron had called a few days earlier and asked to borrow a shirt. He had somewhere to go on Saturday. He never came to get the shirt. I then checked in with Mackenzie to see if she had heard from Cameron that morning. She had. He told her that he was on a college campus south of the city. I looked at the calendar. It was the fourth Saturday of the month; the Saturday for his monthly adopted teen support group. He had gone to A-team meeting.

I called Marion and him, Carl and the Private Investigator headed to the college. Unfortunately, they got stuck in traffic and their arrival was delayed by thirty minutes. They searched all of the rooms in the building. There were no teenagers around. Marion reported their findings and asked me to see if the group had gone on a field trip as they often did. When I checked with one of Cameron's friends who regularly attended A-team meeting, I remembered that it had been moved to the previous week to avoid conflicting with the Memorial Day weekend. They asked the receptionist if he had seen Cameron. He said that he had and that Cameron had left about a half hour earlier. They had missed him again by thirty minutes.

Since the college was on the same side of the city as Ms. Smith's house, they proceeded to her house thinking he might be going there. Before they reached the house, the private investigator had to leave for a previously arranged assignment and the escorts landed at the airport. Upon receiving the escorts' call, Marion and Carl returned to central control to rendezvous with the escorts.

We sat in the family room and mapped out a plan

with the escorts. As they were leaving to implement, I called Ms. Smith remembering that she mentioned the amusement park earlier that week. She told me that, at that moment, Cameron was talking with her daughter Sara. They were planning where they were going to meet. Ms. Smith gave me Sara's cell phone number. When I reached her I discovered that he was at the airport where she worked but she didn't know exactly where. She confirmed her agreement with Cameron and gave me the number he had called her from.

The number was not in the reverse telephone directory. One of the escorts called the number from his out of town cell phone. He attempted to get the male who answered to disclose information that would be helpful to our efforts. However, the male was street wise and was not fooled by the attempt.

The escorts, Carl and Marion went to the amusement park to set up surveillance. I stayed at central control. I called Sara several times to see if she had connected with Cameron. After awhile she no longer answered her telephone indicating that she was in the park where telephones could not be heard.

Suspecting that he also could not contact Sara and that he did not have the twenty-five dollar admission fee, I called Lila's mother. Although she didn't agree with my assessment of Cameron or the program, she had complied with my earlier request to invite Cameron over. Cameron had called earlier to say that he would be there before going to the amusement park at six o'clock. It was almost four o'clock. It appeared that Cameron was not going to make it over to Lila's.

Lila's mother expressed that all she wanted was for Cameron and Lila to spend time together over a quiet dinner.

Unconditional

She felt that if she could talk with Cameron everything would be alright, he would come back home and act right. I didn't bother to tell her that he had run away three times in the last three weeks, been arrested for car theft, run away from the group home and child services, stole his sister's money and car and was currently residing with a drug dealer and his ninety year old blind grandmother. I didn't have the energy and knew it would not change her mind away.

I hung up the telephone and updated Marion who headed to Lila's for surveillance. Before leaving the park, the escorts advised the local police who were stationed at the park of the situation. They agreed, if Cameron showed up, to hold him until the escorts returned. Carl stayed at the park to identify Cameron.

I continued to call random numbers on Cameron's cell phone bill and amazingly pieced together quite a bit of his activities during the previous weeks. He had apparently taken public transit all over the metropolitan area visiting his friends. He rarely visited anyone before he ran away although I would occasionally ask him if he wanted to go visiting. However, over the past year he had either been under punishment most of the time or obligated to his home schooling. Visiting was ruled out.

After approximately an hour, Marion called indicating that he did not believe that Cameron was coming to Lila's. He suspected that someone was trying to pull them off of Cameron's trail. The only one who knew the plan, outside of the people looking for him, was Lila's mother. I called her back to see if I could detect anything from her tone or conversation.

When I called, she said Cameron had not arrived but had called. I asked her to give me the number where he called from. She told me she would call me right back. I was a little surprised when she did and gave me the numbers from where he had been calling over the last few weeks. Most of the time, he had called from Connor's or Ms. Smith's telephones. She also gave me the number where he had called from just a few minutes before. I immediately called Marion and told him that Connor was at Ms. Smith's. Marion and the escorts headed to her house for the second time that day and I, for the first time that day, left the house to pick up Carl from the park. A girlfriend drove so that I did not have to take a car that Cameron would recognize.

When the never lost system announced that they had reached their destination, Marion and the escort couldn't believe their eyes. They were in front of a trailer that had been attached to the ground. In front of the trailer were an abandoned truck and a car up on blocks. On either side of the house for miles in both directions were active, operating industrial buildings. Across the street and behind the house were undeveloped, heavily treed areas. A decrepit storage shed and a well fed lazy dog were on either side of the house. Up until this stop, the escorts had appeared fearless. However, this house which, but for the fact the windows were not boarded or broke, looked like an abandoned house, caused them pause. They requested that Marion go to the door first.

After a short discussion, all three of them exited the car and surrounded the house. One of the escorts knocked on the front door but no one answered. Marion called my cell phone and had me call the house. Since I had called the house a number of times, my number on the caller identification would not arise suspicion. After several rings, the telephone stopped ringing in the middle of a ring as if someone had picked it up. Marion called me and asked me to call again. The same thing happened.

One of the escorts looked in a window and discovered the house was furnished and that a television was playing. Marion, who had not relieved himself all day, moved closer to house to camouflage himself from the street traffic. During the process, he noticed that the side door was pulled together but not completely closed. When he finished, he went over to the door and pushed it open. Someone was inside. Marion took a step in and saw Cameron asleep on the couch. He paused for just a second and then turned around and told the escorts that that was Cameron. Marion then went behind the house so that Cameron would not see him.

The escorts entered the house and walked to either side of Cameron. They asked him if he was Cameron Anderson. Still groggy from his marijuana induced sleep, Cameron responded softly "yes." The escorts told him that his parents had sent them to take him to a program in Utah. After a short conversation, Cameron turned around and the escorts put plastic handcuffs on him. He did not resist the cuffing or strangers taking him away.

Marion had spent the whole day tracking Cameron. In anticipation of the day's ordeal, he had not slept the night before. However, it still pained him to be a part of sending his son away. After they drove off, Marion called to tell me they had apprehended him and asked me to pick him up.

It was too late for Cameron and the escorts to catch the evening flight to Utah. Therefore, they spent the night in a local hotel. To assure that Cameron would not run again, one of the escorts slept on the floor in front of the door. Cameron was quiet and subdued. He cried only while he was alone in the bathroom. The following morning, they flew to Utah.

During the night and through out the trip, the escorts were in constant contact with us. While at the hotel, the escorts reminded us to prepare a letter for Cameron to read on the airplane. With everything that had happened over the last eleven years, especially the last three weeks, Marion and I found it easy to write the following letter to our son. It read:

Cameron:

No matter what you have done or what you may become in the future, we will always love you, unconditionally. Please accept this action as an opportunity for you to become the person I know you can be. Keep God in your life and everything will fall in place.

Love
Mom and Dad.

Cameron read the letter, folded it up and placed it in his pocket.

EPILOGUE

They next day, we visited friends who promised to have us over for a drink after Cameron was placed. As we sat on their back deck over looking their pool, they disclosed to us for the first time in the five years that we had known them, that they too had adopted a hard to place child who had been troubled like Cameron. They tried for two years to assimilate him into their family. However, because of certain medical conditions of the wife, they were forced to return him to the state.

A few days later, still adjusting to Cameron's absence, Marion and I sat quietly eating breakfast. I broke the silence and asked, "What did people mean when they commented on how much we had been through with Cameron? Were they implying that we could have returned him to the state?"

His response expressed my feelings exactly, "I never thought of that as an option. Cameron is our son."

It takes a village to raise a child.

> African Proverb

Coral's Apology

Excerpt from
<u>Grieving a Rollin' Stone</u>

It wasn't the lost of the name that hurt you so bad
It was the lost of a daughter that made you so sad
I lost myself in a sea of pretense
Living out a fantasy

Trying to live in a world where I did not belong
Loving someone who was not my own
Hurting people along the way
Losing myself day by day

I realize now it was more than a name
For my name and my essence are one in the same
But now I am back, set free by death
And never again will I lose myself

© 2005 Shonda Rowe

𝒪n the second day after Rollin' Stone died, Coral woke up feeling better than she had in years. *Damn. I feel like a new woman.* She jumped out of bed and all but floated into the bathroom.

Looking in her vanity mirror, she examined the skin around her eyes, her nose and her mouth. She held her head back and scrutinized the tautness of her chin and her neck. She pulled her jet black, shoulder length hair high in the air letting it fall freely back to her shoulders. Turning her head from side to side, she examined her profile.

"No wrinkles, no crow's feet, no brown spots and no dark circles." She said to the reflection in the mirror.

She stepped in front of the mirrored sliding doors on her now half-filled closet. Pulling the thin straps of her satin nightgown off her shoulders, she allowed it to fall to the floor. Despite the fact that she nursed the twins for six months and pumped for another six, her breasts were still firm and perky. Her narrow waist was at least ten inches smaller than her gently rounded hip. She turned to the side. Her stomach was flat as a board.

"Yeah, I am certainly a sista," she said sliding her hand downward from the small of her back, around a well proportioned hill and stopping at the top of her thigh.

Turning around slowly, she examined every inch of her latté colored body. Then facing the mirror, she looked herself in the eyes as if waiting for the results of the inspection.

After a few seconds of thought, she said, "Juette girl, you still got it. God is good. Juette!" *Where did that come from? I haven't called myself that name in years.*

She pulled back the sliding closet door and spread her clothes into the side that just two days earlier contained Rollin's expensive sweaters, jackets and suits. She noticed a long cotton dress. She loved that dress. Rollin' hated it. He said it looked like a fancy moo-moo that his first wife Pearl might wear. He all but demanded that Coral not wear it.

"I certainly don't want to look like Pearl." She said sarcastically. *What did he used to call her? Matronly, that's it. What an idiot.*

She pulled the dress off the hanger and slipped it on. Looking at herself in the closet door, she admired the sequined head of the African woman on the front of the dress. She ran her fingers over the choker and turban causing the sequins to sparkle in the hint of sunlight peaking around the side of the heavy brocade custom drapery.

She walked towards the sliver of sun and pulled the velvet cord to uncover the sliding glass doors that opened to her private patio. The light that flooded the room was diminished by the dark walls and furnishings. *These drapes, this furniture and this horrible brown wall color were all Rollin's idea. Mental note to self: agenda item number one: redecorate this bedroom. Return it back to wonderful shades of . . . what else? Coral.*

"Now where are my beautiful children?"

She walked out of her bedroom, past the doors to her children's room and her guest room, peaking into each as she moved. The hallway emptied into the main part of the house. She paused in the living room to notice the sunlight shinning through its large picture window and, for the first time that morning enjoyed its unimpeded brightness.

She examined the living room as if she had never seen it before. Rollin' had suggested that she replace the soft coral colored sofa and complimenting chair with a black leather love seat and couch. She had adamantly refused and, of course, that was turbulence. *I certainly don't want to think about that today.*

"You know, this house is beautiful." She said out loud.

Mental Note to self, item two or maybe this should be item one: call parents and thank them for the lovely house and furniture they helped me buy. . . . No, not today. That would cause turbulence. Today is tranquility day; my first step towards a gentler, calmer life. On second thought, thank you to parents, item one on agenda "b" to be executed next week.

Coral walked into the entry hallway that separated the living room from the den. The front door was open. Coral had long since given up on trying to convince Marie that the central air conditioning worked at least as good, if not better than, the little breeze coming through the screen door. Rollin' had pointed that out to Coral. *You know this breeze <u>does</u> feel good and the fragrance from the rose bushes is absolutely divine.*

Coral noticed the large spot of burnt grass on her front lawn. *Why didn't I burn his clothes in the back yard? I must have really been mad. Mental note: item two on agenda "a": call the lawn man. I'm going to need a little . . . no a lot of sod. Mr. Smith, I can't imagine what happened to my lawn.* She smiled to herself and then moseyed into the den.

Sitting in the center of the room, facing the archway, was a large oak heirloom desk, a gift from her grandmother, Juette III. Bookcases filled with medical books, children's books and novels spanned the entire wall behind the desk.

All of them belonged to Coral. She wondered if Rollin' even knew how to read. *He certainly didn't read when he was here, not even to the children. For that matter, neither did I. I can't even begin to count the number of books I bought the kids and me over the last three years. I'd be surprised if I've read even one.*

During the jam-packed years of medical school and her residency, Coral managed to read no less than four books per month. When she started dating Rollin' she never found the time or the peace of mind. She carefully selected four books and placed them on the desk. *Mental Note: item three on agenda "a": read all four books within the next thirty days and read at least one story to the children every night.*

"Now where are those children?"

She quietly pushed open the swinging door leading to the kitchen, pausing in the doorway to watch her children eating breakfast at the counter that separated the kitchen from the bay area that they used as a breakfast nock. Every morning, she was newly amazed at how much alike the twins looked and at how much they each looked like their father. *Rollin' sure made some pretty babies.* Their appearance was truly identical. Yet, their mannerisms, even at three years old, made it clear that Aventa was all girl and Aventurine, Jr. was all boy.

Coral begin singing the twin's favorite tune. "Sweetheart, sweetheart, sweetheart. Will you love me ever? Will you remember the day, when we were sunny and gay? Sweetheart. . . ."

The children squealed when they heard the song. They jumped down from their stools and ran to their mother. Coral fell to her knees and then lay back pretending the children had knocked her down. She wrapped her arms around them and smothered them with kisses.

Unconditional

Marie interrupted their jolly moment when she asked, "Are you having your usual black coffee with artificial sweetener this morning?"

"I feel wonderful. I think I'll go for broke and have whatever the children are having. Let's see."

Coral lifted the twins from the floor, one in each arm, and placed them back on the stools. She sat between and looked in their bowls.

"Okay, I guess it will be cereal with bananas, whole milk and sugar."

Marie had been with Coral since the day the twins came home from the hospital. She tended to the kids, kept the house clean and had meals ready on time. She was never sick and rarely took a day off. As a bonus, she taught the children to speak Spanish. Coral was proud of the fact that her children were the only bilingual kids at the Catholic preschool they attended. *Too bad they aren't the only Stones.*

Coral suspected that Marie knew about the turbulence that Coral had masqueraded as a marriage. She was certain that even in her basement apartment, Marie heard every argument that Coral had with Rollin' and with her parents. However, Marie never made any comments about the situation. *What more can I ask for?*

Everyday, whether Rollin' slept in the house or not, Marie asked, "Will the Mr. be eating breakfast?"

Coral wasn't expecting that question this morning. When it came, she froze. Until that very moment, it had not occurred to her that neither Marie nor the children knew that Rollin' was dead. The only person she had told was Rollin's brother Carney.

I didn't tell them why I was going to the hospital the other night. They probably thought I went to see a patient. They were asleep when

I returned. Yesterday, I was consumed with lunch with my wife-in-law and the burning. I barely spoke to any of them; quick good morning and no good night kisses. Mental note: priority item: spend more times with your children.

But for now, how do I explain to the twins that their father is dead after acting so happy? I certainly can't tell them that their father's death is the source of my elation. Damn it! Turbulence!

She walked out of the kitchen without saying a word. Without notice, she passed the living room, walked down the hallway and into her bedroom closing the door behind her. The diminished ray of sun coming through the sliding glass doors now hurt her eyes. She pulled the drapes close without using the cord.

During these periods of intense turbulence, of which there had been many over the past three years, she yearned to talk with her mother. Before she became a smart ass adult, her mother had been her best friend. They talked several times a day, for any reason or for no reason at all. Even when they disagreed, her mother was always there for Coral, always giving advice and support.

Changing my name started the break down in my relationship with my parents. Although I never asked her, I'm sure it devastated my mother. Why did I do that?

"The name 'Juette' is so important to our family. How could you just throw it away?" Her mother exclaimed when Coral showed her mother the court order.

"Juette one, two, three, four, five. Who really gives a damn?" Coral said snatching the order from her mother's hand, storming out of the house and driving at record speed back to Detroit from Philadelphia.

But now that she was sitting in her bedroom, hiding from her own children the fact that she was happy to be a widow; she couldn't believe how cruel she had been to her mother. *There was no good reason. Actually, there wasn't a reason at all.*

But she had a reason for the pain she inflicted on her parents by her pregnancy and marriage to Rollin'. *At the time, I loved that man. If he had asked, I would have drank his dirty bath water.* She remembered the day she persuaded Rollin' to come over and accidentally on purpose forgot to insert her diaphragm. *I'm a doctor. I know when I'm ovulating.* Knowing her parents would not approve, she waited until after the quiet home ceremony to make the announcement.

Her parents were livid when she told them. Because they loved her, they made an effort to at least tolerate the circumstances. However, when the twins were born and Coral refused to name the first girl of that generation Juette, the relationship crack all but became a clean break. *How many times did I promise her I would? Why did I break that promise?*

"Juette, you have to name the girl 'Juette'. You just can't name those children after that thug, that criminal," her mother had exclaimed. *I can't believe I got so mad at her for calling a thug and a criminal, a thug and a criminal.*

When Coral filled out the birth certificate, she made it official that the girl's name was Aventa Topaz Stone. Her mother, who had come to Detroit planning to stay for six weeks, left the hospital and went directly back to Philadelphia.

"You've hired Marie. She can help you. No matter what, please remember I do now and will always love you, unconditionally," her mother said as she left.

Rollin' was nowhere around.

During the first year of the twin's life, Coral did not speak with either of her parents. She missed them and would send them cards and pictures of their grandchildren. Her mother would always send back a nice, formal, hand written thank you note signed "Love, Juette IV." *I don't need them anyway. I got a career, a husband and two children. She just has to realize that the hierarchy in my life has changed.*

For the twins first birthday, Coral planned a quiet family day on Belle Isle Park. She arranged not to be on call and, surprisingly, Rollin' agreed to go with them. That morning as she packed the car, she noticed a long black Lincoln Continental with Pennsylvania license plates heading towards her house. *Is that? No! I don't believe it.*

The car turned into her driveway and out jumped her father, mother and brother dressed and ready for a picnic.

"What are you doing here?"

"We're here to celebrate the twins first birthday." Her brother responded.

"How? Why?"

"We called last week to tell you we were coming. Marie answered the telephone and told us about family day in the park. I think she wanted to make sure she would get the day off. We drove in last night and stayed with one of my friends from college so that we could surprise you this morning." Her father said.

"Well you certainly did. You even got the big head to come." She said as she hugged her now six feet, five inches tall brother. "Are you going to be the first black player in the NBA?"

Coral didn't hug her mother or her father and they didn't try to hug her. Her parents barely spoke to Rollin'. Eventually, everyone got in their respective cars and drove to the park. The day was civil and everyone, including Rollin' acted courteously. Although her mother didn't ask, Coral

Unconditional

shared a few experiences about the children's first year. In response to each her mother smiled and said, "That's nice."

Her father and brother couldn't seem to get enough of holding and playing with Aventurine, Jr. For most of the day, her mother sat on a blanket in a soft patch of grass and held Aventa quietly in her lap. Aventa played with her dolls and combed her grandmother's hair. Coral noticed her mother steal a kiss from Aventa when she thought Coral wasn't looking. Rollin' just sat off to the side by himself. At the end of the day, her parents and brother got back into their car and left for Philadelphia from the park.

From that day on, her parents called at least once a week and visited at least once a month. Her mother never asked any questions about Rollin'. She never invited Coral to bring the children to the family homes in Philadelphia or Martha's Vineyard. She seemed content to sit and hold Aventa and occasionally steal a kiss from the very energetic Aventurine, Jr.

Thank God, my parents love their grandchildren. Otherwise they would surely disown me. No wonder. I've hurt them so much and I never apologized. I never did any thing to make the relationship better. At least they took the first step. I've spent the last two years engaging in idle small talk. Why would anyone discuss the weather with their mother? Maybe Rollin' wasn't the only idiot in this house. I am so sorry. Mental note: implement agenda "b" today.

Coral was standing in front of a door covered by heavy drapes. *Why am I standing here?* She walked to the nightstand and reached for the telephone but pulled her hand back before picking it up. She sat on the bed. *This is going to be hard.* She took in a big breathe of air; then blew it out slowly. She reached for the telephone again. This time she picked it up and dialed.

She didn't know what she was going to say to her parents or how she was going to say it, but she did know how she was going to start the conversation. When she heard her mother's voice, tears formed in her eyes.

"Hello mother. This is Juette V."

"Your great-great-grandmother picked that name the day her husband bought her freedom. ... She picked it to honor her grandmother who died on the slave ship."

From *Grieving a Rollin' Stone* © 2006

But the greatest of these is love.

1 Corinthians 13:13

Jordan, We Love You Unconditionally.

1 CORINTHIAN 13

¹If I speak in the tongues of men and of angels, but have not love, I am only a resounding gong or a clanging cymbal.

²If I have the gift of prophecy and can fathom all mysteries and all knowledge, and if I have a faith that can move mountains, but have not love, I am nothing.

³If I give all I possess to the poor and surrender my body to the flames, but have not love, I gain nothing.

⁴Love is patient, love is kind. It does not envy, it does not boast, it is not proud.

⁵It is not rude, it is not self-seeking, it is not easily angered, it keeps no record of wrongs.

⁶Love does not delight in evil but rejoices with the truth.

⁷It always protects, always trusts, always hopes, always perseveres.

⁸Love never fails. But where there are prophecies, they will cease; where there are tongues, they will be stilled; where there is knowledge, it will pass away.

⁹For we know in part and we prophesy in part,

¹⁰but when perfection comes, the imperfect disappears.

¹¹When I was a child, I talked like a child, I thought like a child, I reasoned like a child. When I became a man, I put childish ways behind me.

¹²Now we see but a poor reflection as in a mirror; then we shall see face to face. Now I know in part; then I shall know fully, even as I am fully known.

¹³And now these three remain: faith, hope and love. But the greatest of these is love.

About the Author

In 2002, Ms. Whiting began writing the Stone Trilogy. However, during the process, she was confronted with what she calls her blessed season of challenges. The raw emotions of those experiences motivated her to write this collection of inspirational stories. Drawing on writing skills derived from practicing fifteen years as a transactional attorney, she was able to weave her emotions and spirituality into these tightly written, fast moving stories.

Unconditional is her debut book and the first publishing of her endeavor into fiction and creative non-fiction. In the summer of 2006, she will complete the first installment of the highly anticipated Stone Trilogy, *Grieving a Rollin' Stone* © 2006. The trilogy is influenced by the life and death of her father, a notorious Detroit gangster, bigamist, and abuser. *Grieving* will be followed by the sequels, *Semi Precious Stone*©2007 and *Diamond in the Rough*©2008.

Ms. Whiting is a native of Detroit and a graduate of Cass Technical High School and Wayne State University. She completed Georgia State University Law School in Atlanta where she continues to practice law. She is a member of Alpha Kappa Alpha Sorority, Inc., the Atlanta Chapter of Jack and Jill of America, Cascade UMC Church, and the Lovely Ladies of Atlanta. She resides with her husband, is the mother of two children, Ryan and Jordan, and the grandmother of Carter Wilson Clay.

http://home.comcast.net/~nyckiwhiting1/love.html